William Blake *Poet and Painter*

"*I know myself both Poet & Painter*"
— *Blake*

William Blake

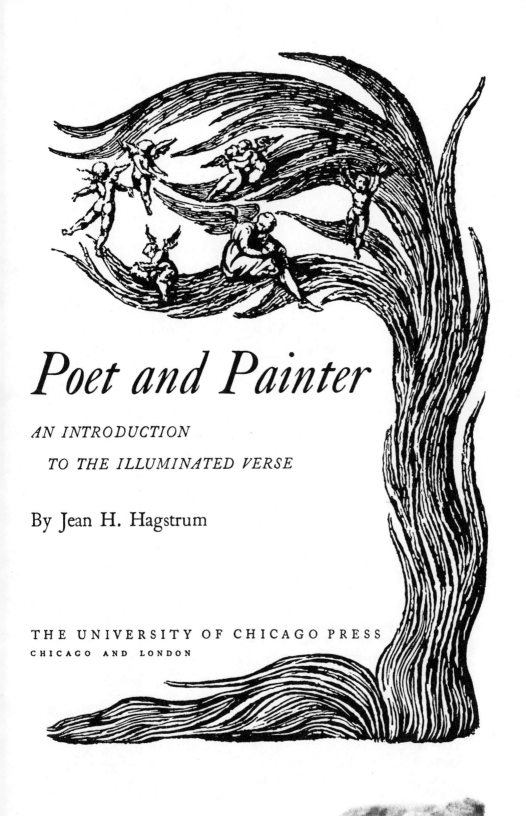

Poet and Painter

AN INTRODUCTION

TO THE ILLUMINATED VERSE

By Jean H. Hagstrum

THE UNIVERSITY OF CHICAGO PRESS
CHICAGO AND LONDON

The University of Chicago Press, Chicago 60637
The University of Chicago Press, Ltd., London

© 1964 by The University of Chicago
All rights reserved. Published 1964
Phoenix Edition 1978
Printed in the United States of America

82 81 80 79 78   9 8 7 6 5 4 3 2 1

ISBN: 0-226-31297-6
LCN: 64-13950

TO RUTH

Preface

This book is intended to be no more than what its subtitle calls it, an *introduction* to Blake's illuminated verse. Part I, on the background of Blake's union of word and design, does not aim primarily to establish sources but to provide a context that will help us define Blake's distinctive art and prepare us to understand and appreciate it. The discussion of the emblem and of illumination, for example, is justified chiefly for generic, not genetic, reasons. Books of emblems and illuminated manuscripts did doubtless contribute visual motifs, but it is more important for my purpose that Blake's works *are* illuminations and emblems.

Part II surveys Blake's composite art from the earliest stereotypes of 1788 to the Job illustrations of 1821–26. I am sure no one will have expected me to discuss every designed page or every illustration, and it should be obvious that an analysis of the unilluminated verses or of separate paintings or of Blake's mythic system lay outside the scope of this study. But two large omissions require explanation: there is no discussion of *Vala, or the Four Zoas,* or of the Dante illustrations, both of which can be regarded as composite art. Although the manuscript of *Vala* in the British Museum bears illustrations, this work was never finally prepared for publication, and as a work of composite art it is not complete and not canonical. A fuller study than this one would of course have included it; it is surely as relevant to a complete understanding of Blake's artistic method as it is to an analysis of his myth. But the complexities of discussing the relation of manuscript design to text were such that I decided to omit this fascinating work from a study concerned primarily with finished masterpieces. The important and difficult task of analyzing *The Four Zoas* is handsomely served by the magnificent facsimile edition recently published by Professor G. E.

Bentley, Jr. The Dante illustrations are also incomplete and were excluded when it was decided to terminate analysis with Blake's last completed work, the designs for the Book of Job. Besides, Professor Albert S. Roe's cogently analytical study, *Blake's Illustrations to the Divine Comedy* (Princeton, 1953), makes further commentary unnecessary.

To have discussed every work in Blake's large corpus would, from my point of view, have been unwise even if it had been possible. Valuable though the long commentaries on Blake are—and every scholar will recognize my debt to my predecessors—it seemed to me that a pioneer study of Blake as a poet-painter ought to provide an overview of Blake's canonical works and give clear hints to the student on how to proceed alone. I have therefore risked being superficial in order to be synoptic and have tried to avoid excessively elaborate commentary that could deter the beginner. I have ventured some detailed analyses—of *Thel*, *America*, and *Job*, for example— but these are intended not so much to establish an interpretation or to illustrate Blake's philosophy as to recommend a method of reading that takes account of all elements of Blake's form—border, design, and word. These Blake himself united, and what Blake hath joined together let no man put asunder!

For most students the approach recommended and followed in this book will be a new experience. I hope the confrontation of Blake's entire form is timely. The publication of the Trianon Press facsimiles by the William Blake Trust—"almost forgeries," as Sir Geoffrey Keynes concedes—is making the true and complete Blake more widely known than ever before in history. My survey will be of most help to those who scrutinize the works that have already appeared in this series: *Jerusalem* (n.d.), *Innocence* (1954), *Innocence and Experience* (1955), *Urizen* (1958), *Visions of the Daughters of Albion* (1959), and *The Marriage of Heaven and Hell* (1960). When these magnificent reproductions are not at hand, others must be made to serve. It is too late now only to "read" William Blake.

For many fraternal and scholarly favors and for reading the entire manuscript I am indebted to Gerald E. Bentley, Jr., and David Erdman. I am equally grateful to colleagues at Northwestern University who have performed the same service: Richard Ellmann, Zera Fink, and Robert Mayo. Subventions from the Northwestern

Graduate School, under Dean Moody Prior, and from the American Philosophical Society made research for this volume possible. The staffs of the following libraries, among many others, spared no effort to bring Blake and the scholar together: the Huntington Library, the British Museum (especially the Department of Prints and Drawings), the Newberry Library, and the Northwestern University Library. Finally, I wish to thank Miss Flora Strohm, who typed the entire manuscript twice, for courteous and efficient assistance.

JEAN H. HAGSTRUM

Contents

Introduction

General Knowledge is Remote Knowledge; it is in Particulars that Wisdom consists & Happiness too.... I intreat, then, that the Spectator will attend to the Hands & Feet, to the Lineaments of Countenances; they are all descriptive of Character, & not a line is drawn without intention, & that most discriminate & particular. As Poetry admits not a Letter that is Insignificant, so Painting admits not a Grain of Sand or a Blade of Grass Insignificant—much less an Insignificant Blur or Mark.

Blake, "A Vision of the Last Judgment"

CHAPTER I

Blake's Form

The time has come to ask whether we can properly assess Blake's intentions or respond appropriately to his art if we confine our attention to his words alone in interpreting a form that consists of words, designs, and borders, integrally combined.

With but few exceptions [1] contemporary commentators have deserted one of the earliest insights into Blake's art—that he "interwined" painting and poetry so closely "that they cannot well be separated" [2] and that in ordinary publication Blake's verses, lacking the support of design, sometimes sound like nonsense.[3] Modern students have usually ignored the visual side of Blake either because they regard it hostilely—"a medium's scribble" [4]— or because it seems intrusive or irrelevant. Some have said that the design brings relief from a portentous text—a function that can hardly have been intended by the poet—while others have considered the paintings as an overflow of Blake's thoughts or even as rival works of art bearing only a casual relation to what the words say.[5]

BLAKE'S UNION OF THE ARTS

It is not hard to imagine what Blake would have thought of criticism that neglected essential elements of his form. He paid a

[1] The most important is Northrop Frye, "Poetry and Design in William Blake," *Journal of Aesthetics & Art Criticism* (September, 1951), pp. 35–42.

[2] Allen Cunningham, "Life of Blake" (1830), reprinted in Arthur Symons, *William Blake* (London, 1907), pp. 396–97.

[3] Edward Quillinan's comment, quoted in Geoffrey Keynes, *Blake Studies* (London, 1949), p. 104.

[4] J. Bronowski, *William Blake* ("A Pelican Book" [Harmondsworth, 1954]), p. 17 (1st ed.; London, 1944).

[5] See Robert Gleckner, *The Piper and the Bard* (Detroit, 1959), pp. 315–16; D. J. Sloss and J. P. R. Wallis, *William Blake's Prophetic Writings* (Oxford, 1926), II, 120–21; Laurence Binyon, *The Engraved Designs of William Blake* (London, 1926), p. 28.

high price to create his illuminated pages—in time, money, patronage, friendship, and spiritual energy. As client and patron languished, Blake neglected his profession as an engraver for his calling as a prophet and gave to each canonical page an enormous labor of mind and muscle. The text was thickly lettered in a varnish impervious to acid on a paper coated with gum arabic. That paper was then soaked, laid face down on a heated copperplate, and rolled under pressure. (The back of the paper may also have been rubbed with an agate burnisher.) The paper being removed, the letters were transferred in reverse to the copper, where they were given such retouching as was necessary. The design may sometimes have been transferred with the text but was more frequently drawn in varnish directly on the plate. The surface of the metal was then treated in a solution that ate away the unvarnished portions, leaving design and letter in low relief. Ink and color were delicately transferred to the etched block from the smooth metal surface of another block against which it was pressed. Proof on "beautiful wove paper" was then taken, and additional color and highlights added. No two copies being alike, color was changed with each issue. Over and around the basic lines such profound alterations were sometimes wrought that one version may differ from another as widely as the work of two artistic schools.[6]

Blake's design may often have been created after the words; some of the *Songs of Innocence* appeared first as unadorned verses in "An Island in the Moon." But priority did not always lie with the words. The manuscript text of *Vala* is accompanied by manuscript design, and on the late Genesis fragment pencil sketches are coincident with the penciled text and suggest that the page was planned from the very beginning to include all its elements.[7] But even if the design usually followed the poem in time, the order of composition alone does not give us license to regard any one element as an afterthought.

Blake treated his method of illumination with reverence and said of it in 1793 that it produced a style "more ornamental, uniform,

[6] Ruthven Todd, "The Techniques of William Blake's Illuminated Printing," *Print*, VI (1948), 53–64.

[7] The Huntington Library possesses eleven leaves that form the beginning of an illustrated manuscript copy of Genesis. For a description and reproductions, see C. H. Collins Baker, *A Catalogue of William Blake's Drawings and Paintings in the Huntington Library* (San Marino, Calif., 1957), pp. 40–43, Plates XXXII, XXXIII.

and grand, than any before discovered."[8] Although he thought that the process had been revealed to him by his dead brother Robert,[9] it had in fact been quite precisely anticipated by Alexander Browne in the seventeenth century.[10] Whatever its source, Blake honored his art with the absorbing devotion of a long life. "I curse & bless Engraving alternately, because it takes so much time & is so untractable, tho' capable of such beauty & perfection."[11] That art, at once so arduous and satisfying, Blake regarded as a seamless unity. Though he once printed off for a friend designs from poems without the text, he apologized for the truncation. "For they when Printed perfect accompany Poetical Personifications & Acts, without which Poems they never could have been Executed."[12]

As early as 1784 or 1785, in "An Island in the Moon," Blake described "Illuminating the Manuscript" as a process in which the writing would be engraved instead of printed and in which a page of text would alternate with a highly finished print. That method Blake was not to follow consistently, but it remained characteristic of his prophetic books, where full pages of design often interrupt the text. Engraved illumination early became an important metaphor in Blake's writings: "*grave* the sentence deep," cries the prophetic speaker in "The Little Girl Lost" as he foretells the Earth's awakening. Illuminated writing Blake must have regarded as his chief means of improving sensual enjoyment and of frustrating Urizen, under whose reign the senses have become shrunken and useless. While Blake was still of the Devil's party—and, unlike Milton, knew it—he saw a demon writing on a rock by means of corroding fires, *engraving* the truth that every bird in his flight opens an immense world of delight otherwise closed to our senses. Urizen, Hecate, Jehovah, and the keepers of the Establishment were represented by the book or by the tablets of law (Plate I). But Los, like Blake himself, is a worker in metal, an artist who draws lines

[8] *The Complete Writings of William Blake,* ed. Geoffrey Keynes (London, 1957), p. 207. Hereafter referred to as *CW*.

[9] Symons, *op. cit.* (n. 2), p. 363.

[10] *Ars Pictoria* (London, 1675), p. 108. C. H. Collins Baker ("The Sources of Blake's Pictorial Expression," *Huntington Library Quarterly,* IV [April, 1947], 360–64) argues convincingly that some of the plates in this work influenced Blake's paintings.

[11] *CW*, p. 837.

[12] *CW*, p. 867 and n. 2. These designs without text are now in the British Museum and are known as the *Large and Small Book of Designs.*

on the walls of heaven, while Enitharmon, like Catherine Blake, colors them with "beams of blushing love." Milton is a sculptor. The walls of the redeemed Job's house are decorated with engraved or painted representations of his experiences. Christ in *Jerusalem* canopies a couch of repose with gold, jewels, pillars, emblems, and spiritual verses. And the love-inebriated fairy who dictates *Europe* writes his book on leaves of flowers. Of Blake's mythic creatures, only the book-loving Nobodaddy and his victims would have approved the neglect of Blake's color and line and the publication of unadorned words on unadorned pages.[13]

The words of "Infant Joy," standing alone, seem gnomic and incomplete, the violin part only of a string trio:

I have no name
I am but two days old
What shall I call thee?
I happy am
Joy is my name
Sweet joy befall thee
Pretty Joy!
Sweet Joy but two days old.
Sweet Joy I call thee:
Thou dost smile
I sing the while
Sweet joy befall thee.[14]

The words alone introduce only two speakers, the child and the mother. The presence in the design (Plate XLIII) of an unsuspected third figure, whose hands are raised in awe, adds dramatic ambiguity —but also makes the scene both an Annunciation and a Holy Birth. The text alone has no suggestion of stem, leaf, or flower—important details, for the flame-flower and the pendant bud suggest sexual experience and birth, and the spiny stem and angular leaves anticipate the world of Experience. The whole page—but not the denuded, ambiguous words alone—provides a precise parallel to Enitharmon's reviving song over the lifeless form of Los:

Arise, you little glancing wings & sing your infant joy!
Arise & drink your bliss!

[13] *CW*, pp. 62, 112, 150, 236, 237, 332, 502, 677.
[14] *CW*, p. 118.

6

For everything that lives is holy; for the source of life
Descends to be a weeping babe. . . .
I wake sweet joy in dens of sorrow & I plant a smile
In forests of affliction,
And wake the bubbling springs of life in regions of dark death.[15]

The design and border of "Infant Joy" enlarge its meaning. The visual details that accompany the Epilogue to *The Gates of Paradise* restrict the meaning and make it more precise.

Truly, My Satan, thou are but a Dunce,
And dost not know the Garment from the Man.
Every Harlot was a Virgin once,
Nor canst thou ever change Kate into Nan.

Tho' thou art Worshipd by the Names Divine
Of Jesus & Jehovah: thou art still
The Son of Morn in weary Night's decline,
The lost Traveller's Dream under the Hill.[16]

It is a safe guess that the last line—like the "dark Satanic mills" or "the tear is an intellectual thing"—has evoked powerful response quite apart from its meaning in the poem or in the context of Blake's thought. Interpreted on the analogy of "Ah! Sunflower," the dream under the hill has been thought of as paradisiacal—as a dream of "that sweet golden clime/Where the traveller's journey is done." But the engraved plate, on which a sooty, bat-winged Satan hovers over the body of the sleeping poet-traveler and is connected to the sleeper's head by a black line, shows that the dream is a Urizenic nightmare (Plate II).

The sleeping form is in fact dominated by one of Blake's firmest symbols of the neoclassical Establishment, the bat. Sometimes, as in the following piece of youthful insolence, the bat symbolizes the literary Establishment,

[15] *Vala, or the Four Zoas* ii. 364–67, 371–73, *CW*, p. 289.

[16] *CW*, p. 771. The source of Blake's first line seems to be the last in Edward Young's *Night* viii: "Satan, thy master, I dare call a dunce." See H. M. Margoliouth, "Blake's Drawings for Young's *Night Thoughts*," *Review of English Studies*, N.S. V (Jan., 1954), 50.

> Lo the Bat with Leathern wing
> Winking & blinking
> Winking & blinking
> Winking & blinking
> Like Dr. Johnson.

Again, it may stand for the regnant philosophy of empirically based unbelief:

> The Bat that flits at close of Eve
> Has left the Brain that won't Believe.

Again, it may represent churchly authority, as in *Europe*, where an ecclesiastic sits on a cloud, wearing a tiara, a Urizenic book open on his knees, and bat-wings spread behind him in front of the Gothic façade (Plate III; cf. Plates LIX, LX). In his *Descriptive Catalogue* of 1809—that angry document of Blakean aesthetics—the painter refers to the "narrow blinking eyes" of the official academicians who have "too long governed art in a dark corner."[17]

The designs that accompany Blake's words always have a function to perform, large or small. Sometimes they make meaning more precise; sometimes they widen the imaginative resonance. Except when Blake has failed of his purpose, they serve an important aesthetic or semantic aim.

UT PICTURA POESIS

For all his dazzling originality, Blake can be regarded as the classical embodiment of those venerable conventions of Western art, pictorial poetry and poetic painting—in fact, of the entire tradition that for centuries had united the visual and verbal arts. That tradition had counted Homer's shield of Achilles as its archetype in poetry, made the Horatian tag *ut pictura poesis* its motto, and left its mark on the greatest literary geniuses of all epochs since ancient times. It had, in spite of the attacks of Lessing and Burke, become a cornerstone of both neoclassical and preromantic aesthetics.[18] Blake's spectacular uniting of the arts owes much to the prestige of such critical commonplaces as this: that poetry "never appears more lovely, than when she dresses herself in the beauties

[17] *CW*, pp. 54, 431, 563.
[18] See Jean H. Hagstrum, *The Sister Arts* (Chicago, 1958).

of painting" and that painting is "never so transporting, as when she emulates the flights, and catches the images of poetry."[19] That statement, made three years after Blake was born, might have been the motto for an age that produced galleries of paintings illustrating Shakespeare and Milton, raised the number of book embellishments to flood proportions, established the English school of visual art, developed aquatint engraving, and stimulated, as never before, the collaboration of the sister arts. Goethe approved Tischbein's notion that poets and painters should daily co-operate in order to secure the perfect unity that neither art alone could attain.[20] Blake's fashionable patron, William Hayley, recalls that during the early years of his friendship with Romney ("whose spiritual aid," Blake said in 1804, "has not a little conduced to my restoration to the light of Art") he and Romney formed many projects for uniting poetry and design.[21]

Blake would have affirmed the doctrine of that arch-pictorialist of the early eighteenth century, Jonathan Richardson, who said that painting was but "another language, which completes the whole art of communicating our thoughts."[22] For, quite apart from the monumental fact that his canonical works consist overwhelmingly of composite art, Blake gives many signs of standing squarely in the pictorialist tradition. In the manner of the Renaissance artist he uses the association of the two arts to elevate painting to the level of poetry—to its "proper sphere of invention and visionary conception": "Poetry consists in these conceptions; and shall Painting be confined to the sordid drudgery of fac-simile representations of merely mortal and perishing substances . . . ?" Even the poems that remain unillustrated are, in texture and ordering, fully pictorialist—graphically imagined and scenically arranged. The unilluminated *French Revolution* indicts the *ancien régime* in one grotesquely and visually conceived emblem after another: a den named Horror contains a man whose soul is a serpent; a tower named Darkness conceals a man wearing an iron mask; in a tower named Bloody a

<hr>

[19] Daniel Webb, *An Inquiry into the Beauties of Painting* . . . (London, 1760), pp. 130–31. "Webb est le plus littéral des interprètes anglais du *ut pictura*" (A. Lombard, *L'Abbé du Bos* [Paris, 1913], p. 347).

[20] Entry for November 7, 1786 (Rome) in *Goethe's Travels in Italy* ("Bohn's Standard Library" [London, 1885]), p. 121.

[21] William Hayley, *The Life of George Romney Esq.* (Chichester, 1809), p. 78; *CW*, p. 852.

[22] "Theory of Painting," *Works* (London, 1792), p. 6.

worm creeps within a skeleton; in a cave named Religion a sick woman lies on a pallet of straw while seven birds of prey feed on her body—and so through seven emblematic scenes, verbal-pictorialist allegories that could easily be transcribed by the illustrator's pencil. Similarly, an unengraved poem in the Rossetti Manuscript attacks the worldly degradation of established religion, not by narrative sequence, logical statement, or angry cry, but by a powerful visualization: a huge serpent breaks the golden gates of a chapel that has deterred the weeping worshipers from entering, and stretches its slimy length up to the altar where it vomits its poison on the sacred elements.[23]

Blake's words are visual, his paintings literary and conceptual. Both word and design show precisely the influence of the pictorialist tradition that also nurtured the imagery of Thomson, the Wartons, Collins, and Gray. Blake's illustrations of Milton, Gray, Young, and Blair reveal that he read these poets as the eighteenth century wanted them read, for he translated their pictorial personifications into visual forms. His illustration of Gray's "To Spring" riots with the very natural and allegorical personifications that appear as the poet's images. Milton is interpreted as the pictorialist school of the Wartons would have wished. Blake's pencil makes the "Mirth" of *L'Allegro* a figure of the Florentine *quattrocento*, surrounded with a group of subordinate figures, all derived from the verse, that dance on the ground and in the air. Melancholy, from *Il Penseroso*, is a statuesque figure, larger than life. She is dressed in black gauze, her eyes are raised heavenward, she is accompanied by the subordinate personifications of the text—a visualization that strikingly corresponds to the way in which Milton's devotee William Collins imagined his personifications, particularly the chaste Evening of his loveliest poem (Plate IV).

BLAKE'S COMPOSITE ART

Blake's commitment to art is one of the firmest in the history of English culture. The only kind of education he approved was the cultivation of imagination and of the fine arts.[24] But he was in no way an aesthete trying to make pink purple. His art rested on moral,

[23] *CW*, pp. 135–36, 163, 576.
[24] Symons, *op. cit.* (n. 2), p. 262.

religious, and philosophical foundations. However neoplatonic he seemed at times to be, he did not really believe that aesthetic form had descended from heaven to endow the work with supernal permanence. Aesthetic form was hammered out in cultural and intellectual struggle and bore the value as it bore the stamp of its creator's mental fight.

Blake's gods and demons create artistic forms that reveal their creators' essential being and meaning. Mathematic form was produced by that arch-rationalist and empiricist Urizen, the creator of Greek temples, round arches, and the whole neoclassic Establishment (Plate I). But Gothic form—the artistic equivalent of "the Forgiveness of Sins"—was the work of Los and Christ and prefigured the redemption of man and society.

Gothic was living form, because of what it expressed and also because of what it was in and of itself. Its parts constituted an organic unity that produced simultaneity of effect. "Every Poem," Blake said, "must necessarily be a perfect Unity; . . . when a work has Unity, it is as much in a Part as in the Whole"; "minutely Appropriate Words" must be accompanied in the design by "minutely Appropriate Execution."[25] His practice showed that he heeded his own precept. In his best work—his failures should not be allowed to measure his aesthetic ideals—there is the pulse of life in all the constituent elements of his composite form, sometimes even in the minutest details of border and scene.

The living unity of Blake's art is less apparent when common motifs are repeated from part to part than when they are treated contrapuntally and when each part makes an original and independent, though of course relevant, contribution. That is, vital coherence *may* indeed be discernible when lamb and boy, tiger and tree, appear in both word and design. But such coherence is incontrovertibly present when the text provides what the design lacks, or when the design provides what the text lacks but what, for its total meaning, it unmistakably requires. An illustration that merely repeats what the words say can be conceived of as purely ornamental in a way that verbal-visual counterpoint cannot possibly be.

On the very plate that contained Blake's praise of Gothic as

[25] *CW*, pp. 596, 778.

living form the etched design surrounding the text illustrates Urizenic "mathematic" form in the dead trunks and roots of trees, the looping snaky lines, and the prone bodies. Even in his first works of illumination, the small, unpretentious twin series produced in 1788 and entitled *There Is No Natural Religion* and *All Religions Are One*, verbal-visual alternation is indisputably present (Plate VB, C, D). The gnomic sentence of each tiny page is accompanied by finely engraved designs and borders. The proverbs either attack the empirical rationalism of Locke, Newton, and the entire eighteenth century, or exalt the human-divine imagination that transcends both sense and reason. Word and design collaborate to blame reason and praise imagination. Thus the words of one of the titlepages state a negative meaning, "There is no Natural Religion." But the design, a Gothic form, implies the antithesis as positively as any words could: There *is* a Poetic and Life-Enhancing Religion of the Imagination. On the titlepage of *The Song of Los* the letters spell LOS, the name of Blake's life-bringing Apollo, but the design, in both figure and landscape, says URIZEN, the name of Blake's life-denying Titan (Plate VI).

Since Blake uses one element of his form to complement another, it follows that no part can be neglected. Reading Blake's illuminated verse in the ordinary text is to use one part of the score only; it is playing a two-handed composition with the right only. Blake's melody often runs from voice to voice: stated in the words, it can be developed in the scene, inverted in the border, and recapitulated in the tailpiece.

As if to enforce the notion that all parts of his form interpenetrate, Blake uses an agitated curved line that moves from top to side, from side to text, from design to border—with unrelenting thrusts toward visual unity, up, down, across the entire page. On the second page of "The Ecchoing Green" (Plate XXXV) a bunch of grapes is handed by a boy in the right-hand border to a girl in the scene at the bottom. In *The Song of Los*, as a serpent threads its colorful but sinister length through the loops of AFRICA at the top, a dragon spits fire into the text from the right border, while between the first and second stanzas a naked boy sleeps by a wooly ram. In "A Dream" Blake responds to the metaphor of his own first lines— "Once a Dream did weave a shade / O'er my Angel-guarded bed" —by tracing delicate shades of vegetation over the top and side of the page. On the page entitled ASIA in *The Song of Los* the text prophesies that frightened kings, driven from their palaces by revolution, will call upon their master Urizen and his priests and councillors to join them in reimposing restraints on their people (Plate VII). No kings appear on this brilliant page, but their victims do, crouching in the border den at lower right and in the vegetated cave at the top that stands for oppressive society, while above the title letters the hint of liberation to come is carried by small nude bodies that rise from the ground or seem to be sucked headlong into a vortex of flame. Thus does Blake's moving line bear a freight of meaning to every nook and cranny of his page.

Blake's composite form consists of language and design or, more particularly, of (1) *words* that appear as short-lined lyrics, sometimes rhymed; as long-lined prophetic poems, usually in septenary rhythm, never rhymed; and as prose mottoes or aphorisms; and of (2) *designs* that have these constituent elements: (*a*) color, (*b*) border, and (*c*) picture or scene.

1. *Language.*—Blake's sense of grammar and syntax is uncertain, his punctuation is eccentric, and his sentences lack logical connectives. These qualities appear in all the various styles Blake employs —in the highly terse and often obscure epigrams, in the song-like lyrics, and in the allegorical-pictorial prophecies. Each of these verbal manners is related to trends in eighteenth-century language, and each is also intimately connected with the tradition of *ut pictura poesis*, of literary pictorialism.

Blake's love of the epigram, "his genius for crystallization,"[26] which lends a gnomic quality to more than his proverbs, he shared with both an immediate and a more remote circle. His friend Fuseli wrote and translated epigrams, and Fuseli's friend Lavater produced aphorisms that Blake annotated. Blake himself found epigrammatic utterance so natural that he fell into it in his own comments on other people's works. He must have early been exposed to the short and often cryptic sentences that were engraved with emblem and *impresa*. In fact, the association of the epigram with an object of visual art is one of the oldest in the long history of pictorialism: aphorisms appeared under urns, monuments, statues, and paintings in antiquity, and one of the most popular types of ancient epigram

[26] Northrop Frye, *Fearful Symmetry* (Princeton, 1947), p. 5.

was written to accompany an art object. There is abundant and appropriate context for those many works in which Blake engraved mottoes under or around his designs. It is natural that the language of a professional engraver should resemble the posy or *mot* of the engraved page.

Blake's lyrics, which are always more musical than logical, he began to write in childhood, during the ballad revival led by Bishop Percy. He sang his own earliest lyrics in extempore tunes so catching that musically adept people bothered to note them down.[27] Blake's visions often came accompanied with sound—he heard the sound of harps before the sun rose over the ocean at Felpham[28]—and even the elaborate and overwhelming designs of *Jerusalem* cannot hush the singing of the words. Job's redeemed family sing and play on the last plate as Blake unites poetry, painting, and music, the three arts that have survived into the present from man's unfallen state.[29]

Allegorical-pictorial language was so fashionable that Blake could hardly have avoided its impress. Preromantic critics praised the pictorial qualities of the unphilosophical, naïve, and believing Elizabethan writers, and the term *picturesque* referred specifically to the way in which Christian faith personified its meanings.[30] The school of Warton, Collins, and Gray, to which Blake clearly belonged as a young poet, made pictorial personification the chief weapon in its poetic arsenal. Moreover, the pictorialist tradition urged the icons of Ripa, antique statuary, and the paintings of the high Renaissance upon the personifying poet, as guarantees of visual sophistication. Blake's earliest intellectual milieu alerted him to the allegorical persons behind even unvisual language, and when he came to write his own verse he made the verbal allegorical scene one of the chief features of his style. Blake's verse is sometimes baffling because he carries to extreme what has elsewhere been called the

[27] Symons, *op. cit.* (n. 2), pp. 360, 387.

[28] Letter to Hayley, January 27, 1804, *CW*, p. 835.

[29] "Blake's engraved poems . . . present, ideally, a unified vision of the three major arts to the individual as the musical drama, with its combination of speech, sound and setting, presents it to the audience" (Frye, *op. cit.* [n. 26], p. 186). There was ample precedent in the pictorialist tradition for the union of the three arts. Verbal tableaux on the subject of music were often accompanied, literally or figuratively, by the sounds of music. See Hagstrum's discussion of *Alexander's Feast*, which Blake probably did not like, and Gray's *Bard*, which was one of the formative influences on his genius (*op. cit.* [n. 18], pp. 205–6, 306–14).

[30] [Richard Hurd], *Moral and Political Dialogues* (London, 1759), pp. 123–24.

picture-gallery manner of ordering poetic materials—one moves from painting to painting as in a room. Contiguity replaces narration, and imagistic stress replaces logic; it requires a trained act of the historical imagination for such stasis in verbal art not to seem inappropriate and *gauche*.

2*a. Color*.—Heinrich Wölfflin has distinguished between painterly art that stresses chromatic tone and linear art that makes outline basic.[31] Blake, by theoretical conviction and long practice, was a linear artist. Like the neoclassical aesthetician—to whom, in spite of himself, he now and then bears striking affinities—he rated color below line, Venetian painters below Romans and Florentines, harmony below melody, chiaroscuro below outline. For him "the great and golden rule of art, as well as of life" was this: that "the more distinct, sharp and wirey the bounding line, the more perfect the work of art."[32] Such an austere but dedicated linearism—and also, of course, the habit of altering the color to make each copy absolutely unique—have deterred students from interpreting and even responding to Blake's color. But Blake's originals are so incomparably superior to bad reproductions, however clear the line, and the rainbow splendors of the Stirling *Jerusalem* so surpass the black and white austerities, however fine, of the Linnell-Rinder copy that one simply cannot write off color as an irrelevant afterthought sometimes added by Catherine Blake.

Some colors are surely symbolic. The blue in *Jerusalem*, *Milton*, and the *Songs of Experience* stands for Urizenic night, and the brilliant washes that streak the yellows and reds of dawn diagonally across the page of *Milton* presage its climactic apocalypse. Even though individual copies are unique and even though Blake ranges from simple watercolor in pastel shades to all the pomp and richness of illumination in gold, purple, and scarlet, certain colors do remain consistent in all copies. All versions of "The Sick Rose" show the yellowing leaves, though perhaps with differing degrees of emphasis. And even when the color is changed, the intent remains

[31] *Principles of Art History*, trans. M. D. Hottinger (New York, n.d.), pp. 18 ff.

[32] *CW*, p. 585. Joseph Spence (*Crito* [London, 1752], p. 7) is most condescending about color, the lowest virtue of painting but the one that is most appealing to the vulgar. Abraham Rees (*The Cyclopedia; or Universal Dictionary of Arts, Sciences, and Literature* [London, 1819]) calls drawing the "soul of beauty, character, and expression" (article on "Drawing" in Vol. XII).

clear: a red streak can suggest the sunrise as well as a yellow streak, and a halo highlighted with gold means the same as a halo drawn with a dark line around a light space. In fact, the later, more elaborate coloring often points up what should have been an obvious meaning in the simpler coloring: in early versions the green plant of "The Divine Image" and the pink flower of "Infant Joy," whose lines and shapes should suggest flames, are in later versions made unmistakably flame-like by a richer and more varied coloring.

Blake's color serves to heighten meaning, not reduce it, and to emphasize form, not obscure it. It is a vital and indispensable element of his composite art.

2b. Border.—The borders of many engravings contemporary with Blake—light, delicate, and elegant—bear some resemblance to the ornamental designs of his illuminated poems. But while such contemporary borders tend to be frozen into inorganic, stylized shapes, completely separate from what they surround, Blake's stand in an ever changing, highly flexible relation to other elements of his form. As they invade and cross the text, grow out of the title, or support the main designs, they achieve the status of living members of a living body. That status they possess even when they represent the tiniest and humblest forms of natural life.

Blake's range is impressive even in border motifs. He sometimes creates the horrific sublime that he learned from Fuseli and his school and from Milton's gigantic imagination, which loved to disport in interstellar space. But he can also produce the tenderly beautiful and delicate cherished by rococo and preromantic artists alike.

> For Los & Enitharmon walk'd forth on the dewy Earth
> Contracting or expanding their all flexible senses
> At will to murmur in the flowers small as the honey bee,
> At will to stretch across the heavens & step from star to star . . .[33]

Blake's liveliest and most progressive contemporaries constantly appealed to children and primitives, who were thought to possess the picturesque concreteness of imagination the rationalistic Establishment lacked. Blake too believed in the authority and authenticity of "infinite particulars":

[33] *Vala, or the Four Zoas* ii. 295–98, *CW*, p. 288.

> ... not a line is drawn without intention, & that most
> discriminate and particular. As Poetry admits not a Letter
> that is Insignificant, so Painting admits not a Grain of
> Sand or a Blade of Grass Insignificant . . .[34]

The grain of sand that bears within it an infinite world mocks the
mocker and teaches that man, God, and nature are profoundly one.
Just as Isaiah was led by his senses to see the infinite in everything,
so the poetic genius weans man from looking beyond the sky where
Chaos and Ancient Night dwell and teaches him to regard instead
"the little winged fly, smaller than a grain of sand," for

> It has a heart like thee, a brain open to heaven & hell,
> Withinside wondrous & expansive . . .
> > hence it clothes itself in rich array:
> Hence thou art cloth'd with human beauty, O thou mortal man.[35]

Such is the gospel preached by Blake's borders with their tiny
and unpretentious natural life. "Every thing that Lives is Holy."

> A Skylark wounded in the wing,
> A Cherubim does cease to sing.[36]

For Sterne the universe was a great Sensorium; Blake's world
quivers with "the nerves of Joy." His borders, with their tiny but
unique forms of organic life, work against the unitary, legalistic
system of Urizen—his "One command, one joy, one desire, . . .
One King, one God, one Law"—and support the aspiration of all
things to a natural and uninhibited life.[37]

Besides the "glorious spiritual vegetation" of the sons of Los
there is also the world perceived by the decaying "Vegetable Ratio,"
the world made of Urizen's frozen bones, of his nets, gins, rocks,
chains, snow, and ice. Blake's awakened eye perceives that the
infinite is not of one kind only but of two kinds. Both are embodied
in the illuminated borders: in *Innocence* they vibrate with holy life,
in *Experience* they are frozen in Urizenic night. The Urizenic
borders—scanter, severer, deader than the lush borders of joy—
appear everywhere in Blake, with their worms, serpents, bats, loops,

---

[34] "A Vision of the Last Judgment," *CW*, p. 611.
[35] *Milton* i. 27–31, *CW*, p. 502.
[36] "Auguries of Innocence," ll. 15–16, *CW*, p. 431.
[37] *Urizen* ii. 39, 41, *CW*, p. 224. See also *ibid.*, iv, 41, *CW*, p. 228.

spiny stems, oak leaves, exposed roots, decaying tree trunks, and bent, grieving human figures.

Blake's borders thus serve at least two purposes. They invite the imagination to leap from the minute particular to a realm of joy and meaning and of imaginative release. But they also present a spectacle of that to which the human mind, perverted by fear and custom, is often the slave—a cactus land of dying trees and empty men.

2c. Picture and scene.—The pictures of Blake's illuminated books —frontispieces, separate pages without text, or designs, above, below, or in the middle of the text—bear many relations, both subtle and obvious, to the words they embellish. Occasionally they unambitiously reduplicate the verbal scene. More often they are visual translations of Blake's metaphors. More frequently still they represent the personifications created in the poem or required by its meaning. Blake's most characteristic use of illustration is to give visual form to his personifications. Although some of these resemble the bland figures that lurk in the blank verse of the eighteenth-century Miltonists, the best ones are the palpable creatures of Blake's vision, the real persons of his own myth, which he created in preference to being enslaved by another's system and which he fervently bodied forth in prophecy, not allegory.

For Blake there was a stairway of vision, divided, like most things, into four flights.[38] *Single* vision was characteristic of the eighteenth-century rationalists for whom a grain of sand was only and ever a grain of sand. From his earliest engraved work in 1788 to his last, Blake attacked the vision of the empirical rationalist, who could never rise above the earth-bound senses and who inevitably looked upon the imagination as only a combiner of observed data. Single vision saw the sun as a round guinea.

Twofold vision saw it sometimes as a Thomsonian personification, sometimes as a chorus of angels singing "Holy, Holy, Holy is the Lord God Almighty," and sometimes as Los, Blake's own life-bringing Apollo, a precursor and associate of the Artist-Christ. A single visionary saw a thistle on the path, but Blake saw Urizen, who blocked his progress to London and free art. In all cases two-fold vision involves a *persona*—from the Christian or pagan

---

[38] See the letter and poem to Thomas Butts, November 22, 1802, *CW*, pp. 816-19.

tradition, from Blake's own myth—that animates and interprets phenomenal reality.

The *third* kind of spiritual sight is vouchsafed to those who keep the light of vision burning in the darkness of Experience. Such vision is threefold; as in single vision you see the sun; as in twofold you also see Los standing in the sun. But now, through practicing love, the forgiveness of sin, and honest art, you can achieve a personal triumph of the will and a conviction of right purpose. Uproot the Urizenic thistle, and Los will blaze his approval in the sky. Desert the man of measured merriment in Felpham for a prophetic career in London, and a Hallelujah Chorus will fill the bright air.

Blake's highest, the *fourfold*, vision is essentially prophetic, a vision of the future and of redeemed nature and society. It sustains the concluding apocalypses of *Milton*, *Jerusalem*, and *The Four Zoas*, when Christ, replacing Los and Luvah, becomes all in all, when man's warring faculties have been composed, when evil has been redeemed, and the Urizenic dispensation ended. Eden, which is perceived only in this fourth kind of vision, is prefigured in twofold and in threefold vision. But since Eden is a future state not yet attained, it is discerned only by the eye of the mind—a mind capable of a gigantic act of both recollection and faith. For in the highest vision the mind projects and enlarges upon the screen of the future the imagined glories of primal innocence and the real triumphs of life.

As a man with a message, Blake was bound to define poetry as allegory. But as one who believed in the reality of his visions, he was bound to define that allegory as an address "to the Intellectual powers, . . . altogether hidden from the Corporeal [that is, materialistic] Understanding."[39] Blake's quarrel with the neoclassical allegorist was that his personifications were not real, that they were merely the generalizations of reason from sense-data, and that they belonged to what William Collins called the "shadowy tribe of mind." The doyen of neoclassical aestheticians, the Abbé du Bos, had said that "allegorical personages are such as have no real existence, but have been conceived and brought forth merely by the imagination of painters, from whom they have received a name, a body, and attributes."[40]

[39] Letter to Butts, July 6, 1803, *CW*, p. 825.
[40] *Critical Reflections on Poetry, Painting and Music* (London, 1748), I, 152.

From such purely empirical-rational allegory, from such playful and wanton insincerity, the figures of Blake's designs and dreams must be sharply distinguished. No matter that they are often formally distorted and plastically outrageous. No matter either that the scholar can see behind them the traditional portraits and conventional icons of the Western heritage. Blake's strong sense that his symbolic figures were the living persons of a cosmogonic drama gave them a solid flesh that no other personifications of the period possessed. Words alone could not have expressed the authentic particularities of Blake's vision. For words alone had too often abjectly served reason and enforced the life-denying generalizations of neoclassical culture—those "Mountains & Valleys, which are not Real, in a Land of Abstraction where Spectres of the Dead wander."[41]

[41] Letter to Butts, September 11, 1801, *CW*, p. 809.

PART ONE

The Background of Blake's Composite Art

CHAPTER II

The Art Of Illumination

Behind the artistic and philosophical distinction Blake drew between Gothic or living form and Grecian or mathematical form lay one of the profoundest conflicts of his life. Ultimately the medieval won Blake's deepest loyalties, and that victory opened some of the richest veins in his imagination. But the Gothic did not win easily or without conflict. For the poet, like his age, had to confront the revived artistic claims of Roman and Greek antiquity—now given new vigor by exciting exploration and archeological discovery. Blake's ultimate equation of the spectrous fiend who tormented him with that iron-hearted tyrant who had ruined ancient culture[1]— and also his fusion of the Jupiter of the Greeks with the Jehovah of the Jews—achieved the intensity that it did precisely because Blake bore intimate relations to the neoclassical revival in art that everywhere surrounded him.

CLASSICAL ANTIQUITY

Blake was a pictorialist in aesthetic training and predisposition as well as in his own early practice of the sister arts. And pictorialist doctrine had for centuries recommended classical example to both poets and painters and urged them to imitate ancient marbles in idealizing their figures. In the later eighteenth century, pictorialism took a new lease on its old life. As quantities of "Etruscan" vases were dug from classic ground, artists were reminded that Raphael, Giulio Romano, and Nicolas Poussin had used vase paintings as models. The new finds, like the old, were made to support the union of the arts. The dazzling volume that reproduced William Hamilton's collection of urns preached the orthodox message. On one classical design—a ruined block with an Etruscan vase in front

[1] Letter to Hayley, October 23, 1804, *CW*, pp. 851–52.

—appears the Horatian tag, *Ut Pictura Poesis* (Plate VIII). On another block of ancient stone appears its adaptation by Dufresnoy: *Similis Que Poesi sit Pictura*[2] (Plates IX).

Blake's father, who was a hosier and perhaps but little interested in the arts, nevertheless saw to it that the lessons of classical antiquity were not lost on his son. The elder Blake bought for William engravings and models of the famous classical marbles—the Dying Gladiator, Hercules, the Venus dei Medici, and heads, hands, and feet from ancient statues. When very young, he, like his brother Robert, must have drawn from the antique. He was apprenticed to the chief engraver of the first volume of the epoch's most influential book on classical antiquities and had attended the school of Henry Pars, whose brother William had traveled with Chandler and Revett in Asia Minor, doing sketches for the Society of Dilettanti—four of which Blake himself engraved in 1791[3] (Plate X).

Influence from the ancients was mediated to Blake most strongly of all by his intimate personal and professional friendship with two of the most insistently classicizing artists of his day. Along with George Cumberland the Elder he hoped "to renew the lost Art of the Greeks." To his friendship with John Flaxman, whom he addressed as "Dear Sculptor of Eternity" and called "a Sublime Archangel," he credited his ability to "subsist on earth" after his disrupting angelic visions.[4]

Cumberland, himself an author and artist, responded to woodland romanticism, the landscape picturesque, and German sentimentalism as Blake never did; but in many essential matters of taste the men were profoundly united. Blake drew after Cumberland and reduced to engraved plates some of the drawings that Cumberland had made to illustrate his work on aesthetics. (That labor of Blake, Cumberland called in print the condescension of a man of extraordinary

[2] *Collection of Etruscan, Greek, and Roman Antiquities from the Cabinet of the Honorable W. Hamilton* ... (Naples, 1766), II, 4, 5. On the importance of the mottoes from Horace and Dufresnoy see Jean H. Hagstrum, *The Sister Arts* (Chicago, 1958), pp. 9–10, 174–76.

[3] Benjamin Heath Malkin, *A Father's Memoirs of his Child* (London, 1806), p. xix. For a discussion of Robert Blake's sketch book see Collins Baker, *A Catalogue of William Blake's Drawings and Paintings in the Huntington Library* (San Marino, Calif., 1957), pp. 1, 50–51 and Plate XXXVII. On Pars see Geoffrey Keynes (ed.), *The Letters of William Blake* (London, 1956), p. 29 and n.

[4] Letters to Cumberland, August 26, 1799, and July 2, 1800, *CW*, pp. 795, 797; letter to John Flaxman, September 21, 1800, *CW*, pp. 801, 802.

genius, the highest compliment "I believe I shall ever receive.")
Blake also paid Cumberland the compliment of sharing his zeal for
the chaste outline, for the "fine, firm, flowing" line—an aesthetic
principle that Cumberland derived from antique art [5]

Chesterton has said that "Flaxman upside down is almost a
definition of Blake."[6] As a definition the remark is both overly
simple and obscure. Exactly what is an inverted classicist? Blake
certainly shared Flaxman's devotion to precise line and firm outline,
his aversion to chiaroscuro, his habit of borrowing postures from
Michelangelo's Sistine ceiling, his love of literary and allegorical
scenes and of personifications, his flowing representations of aerial
movement and of the commerce of earth and sky, and his use of
emblematic motifs from classical urns and friezes. Blake may even
not have escaped entirely the sweetness that simpers on the faces of
Flaxman's Christs, heroes, Beatrices, and cupids. But Blake, a much
larger spirit than Flaxman, could not have remained content with
the chaste and graceful lines, the depthless surfaces, and the
intellectual slackness of his friend's engravings. Much of Blake's
work Flaxman must have regarded as baroque aberration. Even
though Blake was as insistently a linear artist as Flaxman, he
always used bolder, tauter, more energetic, and more complex lines
than his friend was ever capable of producing.[7]

Blake was thus exposed to antiquity under the most favorable
auspices. The tendency of the age and the pull of intimate friendship made Greece and Rome inescapable. Traces of the ancient
civilizations appear everywhere. The engraved Argument of the
Visions of the Daughters of Albion adapts a recently discovered Roman
painting[8] and shows with what speed Blake responded to a classical

[5] George Cumberland, *Some Anecdotes of the Life of Julio Bonasoni* (London,
1793), p. 26; *Lavinia the Maid of Snowdon: A Tale with Etchings by the Author*
(London, 1793); *A Poem on the Landscapes of Great Britain ... Written in the Year
1780 ... with Etchings by the Author* (London, 1793); *Thoughts on Outline, Sculpture,
and the System That Guided the Ancient Artists in Composing Their Figures and Groupes
...* (London, 1796), pp. 1–8, 19, 47–48.

[6] G. K. Chesterton, *William Blake* (London, n.d.), p. 27.

[7] G. E. Bentley, Jr., "Blake's Engravings and His Friendship with Flaxman," *Studies
in Bibliography*, XII (1959), 161–88. See Flaxman's illustrations, some of which were
engraved by Blake, to the *Iliad* (1805), to the *Odyssey* (1805), to Dante (1807), to
Hesiod (1817). (I give the dates of the editions consulted.) See also Flaxman, *Lectures
on Sculpture* (London, 1838), esp. the accompanying plates.

[8] David Erdman, "Blake's Vision of Slavery," *Journal of the Warburg and Courtauld
Institutes*, XV (1952), 250 and n.

influence. His representation of the eagle carrying the serpent in *The Marriage of Heaven and Hell* recalls the twelfth book of the *Iliad* (ll. 200 ff.). A plausible source for the famous nude in "Glad Day" is a bronze faun recently dug up at Herculaneum.[9] One ancient tomb seems to anticipate Blake's often repeated Door of Death, and another, with the skeleton supine in the center, suggests illustrations for Blair and Young.[10] Blake's kind of drapery, that veils lightly but does not conceal or distort, appears in engravings after the ancients,[11] in the Ashmolean marbles at Oxford, and in the Parthenon friezes, which Blake admired. Blake drew a goat-legged Silenus after the antique, did a series of classical heads for Thornton's *Vergil*, and now and then seems to recall the "Apotheosis of Homer," that group allegory in stone that now stands in the Ephesus Room of the British Museum.[12]

But Blake was a pictorialist preacher, not a pure painter or a pure lyrist; and these classical influences, like all others upon him, did not remain either literary or visual strokes merely but entered his composite art as emblems of meaning and truth. Classical civilization came to stand for war, rationalism, the loss of imagination, and the degradation of prophetic truth to priestcraft and allegory. Greek form was ultimately equated with the mathematical form that resided in the reason and the memory, and the whole horror of Newtonian mechanism and Lockean empiricism Blake finally came to evoke by means of classical symbols.

Those anti-classical habits of thought were arrived at by a long, complex process. Stages in the way are represented by *Tiriel* and *Thel*. One of Urizen's most characteristic poses may have its source in the classical figure of Jupiter Pluvius, the arms extended akimbo being the clouds from which the rain falls.[13] In his early engravings after William Pars, Blake's burin traced violent scenes from mythic warfare[14] (Plate X); and in the illustrations of Roman history that

[9] Anthony Blunt, *The Art of William Blake* (New York, 1959), p. 34.

[10] Hamilton, *op. cit.* (n. 2), II, 56–57; *idem, Collection of Engravings from Ancient Vases . . . Now in the Possession of Sir William Hamilton . . .* (Naples, 1791), I, 24.

[11] See Thomas Martyn and John Lettice, *The Antiquities of Herculaneum* (London, 1773), Plate XX. (This work is a translation of an Italian volume published in 1757.)

[12] See Blake's drawings in the British Museum, Department of Prints and Drawings, LB. 9 (xxvi–xxvii).

[13] Blunt, *op. cit.* (n. 9), p. 41 and Plates 25c, 21a, 21b.

[14] James Stuart and Nicholas Revett, *The Antiquities of Athens*, Vol. III (London, 1792), Plates XXI–XXIV.

appeared in 1798, the four plates engraved by Blake after an anonymous artist all represent moments of violence, oppression, or dramatic death.[15] Rome and War are clearly associated. The mouth of the Greek tragic mask was a regular symbol of oppression and tyranny in both Fuseli and Blake, and Blake's two representations of Corinna parody inspiration—with their masklike mouths, the vacant, Urizenic piety of their gazes, and the feel of death and negation they unmistakably convey.[16]

By 1808, when he illustrated Milton's *Nativity Ode*, the friend of Cumberland and Flaxman, the man who had hailed the coming to Europe of "the immense flood of Grecian light & glory,"[17] struck classical values their *coup de grace*. In the watercolor illustration entitled the "Overthrow of Apollo" (Plate XI) destruction rages in the heavens and on the earth, the mad priestess raves in her cell, nymphs bend in desperation. And the god himself stands above the chaos on a pedestal wrapped in flame and rests his back against a serpent-entwined trunk. His shape is that of the famous Apollo Belvedere, for years the great exemplar of neoclassical idealization, a statue that Flaxman had said embodied more ideal beauty than any other statue whatever.[18] But amid the ultimate apocalyptic destruction, Blake's handsome oracle stands dumb, frozen, and helpless.

GOTHIC ART

Blake attacked classical civilization by sharply contrasting its death and horror with the life-bringing Gothic. "The Classics! It is the Classics, & *not the Goths nor Monks*, that Desolate Europe with Wars."[19] And in the late aphorisms that condemn Grecian

[15] Charles Allen, *A New and Improved Roman History* ... (2nd ed., London, 1798).

[16] See Fuseli's several heads of Oedipus in his Italian Sketch Book (British Museum, Department of Prints and Drawings, 198b5**). See the Corinna heads in Geoffrey Keynes, *Pencil Drawings by William Blake* (London, 1927), Plate 45.

[17] Letter to Cumberland, July 2, 1800, *CW*, p. 797.

[18] John Thomas Smith, *Nollekens and His Times* (London, 1828), I, 246.

[19] "On Homer's Poetry" (*c.* 1820), *CW*, p. 778 (italics added). For commentary on Blake and the classics, see Peter F. Fisher, "Blake's Attacks on the Classical Tradition," *Philological Quarterly*, XL (January, 1961), 1–18; *idem*, "Blake and the Druids," *Journal of English and Germanic Philology*, LVIII (October, 1959), 589–612; Stephen A. Larrabee, *English Bards and Grecian Marbles* (New York, 1943), chap. v. Certainly much of Blake's anti-classical animus arose from the relative position in

gods as diagrams and classic form as mathematical Blake calls Gothic art living form and Eternal Existence. In his own visual symbolism Gothic architectural motifs represent Blake's version of the good as surely as the round arch stands for Urizen and his dispensation.

If classical influence was for Blake inescapable, equally so was the medieval and even more so was the conflict between the two that his age erected into one of its major dialogues. That contrast, in an age of artistic confusion and indecision, must have been borne in on Blake early and vividly. In Mrs. A. S. Matthew's drawing room he saw decorations in the Gothic manner by his classicizing friend Flaxman, who, for all his devotion to antiquity, also loved Italian medieval art and drew motifs from Duccio, the Pisani pulpits, the Campo Santo in Pisa, the West front of the Cathedral at Orvieto, and the frescoes of the Chiostro Verde at Santa Maria Novella in Florence. Stothard, after whom Blake frequently engraved, was now Grecian, now Gothic. John Martin praised both the antique and the medieval. The dining hall at Carlton House combined Gothic columns and Grecian tables and chairs. And Wyatt began as a classicist and ended by creating Fonthill and Ashridge.[20]

Blake's participation in the medievalism of his age began conventionally and superficially but soon generated one of the profoundest influences on his work as poet-painter. His earliest representations of medieval England, as in "Jane Shore" and "Queen Emma," are not without medieval flavor, but their conviction is weakened by reminiscences of Stothard and Angelica Kauffmann and the manner tends to be fashionable and simpering. Neverthe-

---

neoclassical culture of the pagan and the Christian: "Fifteen centuries after the Church Fathers had valiantly routed the pagan deities and their philosophical apologists, Jupiter had returned in triumph to the realms of the most Christian kings of Europe. The Chateau of Versailles was adorned with gracious images of the gods of Greece and Rome, while Christ and the saints were severely restricted to the chapel" (Frank E. Manuel, *The Eighteenth Century Confronts the Gods* [Cambridge, Mass., 1959], p. 3).

[20] Alexander Gilchrist, *Life of William Blake* ("Everyman's Library" [London, 1945]), p. 38 (1st ed.; London, 1863); Margaret Whinney, "Flaxman and the Eighteenth Century," *Journal of the Warburg and Courtauld Institutes*, XIX (July to December, 1956), 269–82; John Steegman, *The Rule of Taste from George I to George IV* (London, 1936), pp. 141, 161.

less, Blake's early labor as Basire's apprentice and Gough's engraver —when he copied the Gothic monuments of Westminster Abbey and other churches and monasteries—was to bear richer fruit than the derivative paintings and drawings of his earliest manner. The Gothic became Blake's steadiest symbol for the good, but it also now and then contributed visual motifs that were pejorative. The spiked iron crown that the Urizenic tyrant so frequently wears may be an adaptation of the venerable English crown of that shape. (Here the disadvantage of being a king overcame the advantage of being medieval.) The stony, supine figures modeled on Gothic funerary art symbolized either poetic fancy frozen under tyranny or the medieval artist's warning of the stony death that awaits the oppressor. Blake's painting and engraving of the Canterbury pilgrimage (similar in style but superior in force to his *Faery Queene* procession) is a masterpiece of neo-Gothic inspiration that resembles those large folded engravings that appeared in works on medieval antiquity and that Blake must have seen often as an apprentice engraver.[21]

Short of the illuminations themselves, Blake's deepest expression of medieval feeling occurs in "The Grey Monk," a ballad from the Pickering Manuscript (*c.* 1803) that was never illuminated. The dying monk, who addresses a dying mother with starving children —all victims of an unnamed tyrant—speaks the word of forgiveness and nonviolence in the moment of martyrdom. His noble defense of the tear, the sigh, the martyr's groan as morally and even ontologic-ally superior to the iron hand of tyranny, which only breeds other tyrants, sprang from Blake's profoundest conviction. On the side of vengeance he regularly placed the Deists, the classics, Voltaire, Rousseau, Gibbon, Hume. On the side of forgiveness and the religion of Jesus, he placed Wesley, Whitefield, the humble monks, and the unknown medieval religious. It is tempting to believe that

21 Blunt, *op. cit.* (n. 9), pp. 7–8; Rossetti MS (British Museum), Add. MS 49460, p. 9; Richard Gough, *Sepulchral Monuments in Great Britain*...(London, 1786; see the edition at the Bodleian Library with MS notes and insertions [Gough Prints 221 and 223a] and the original pencil drawings also in the Bodleian [Gough Maps 225]). For use of spiked crowns by Blake's contemporaries, see the twenty color stipples at the Huntington Library, including those done by Bumbury for Macklin's Shakespeare gallery. See also Blake's "Characters from Spenser's Faery Queen" in Petworth House (Courtauld Institute Negative: No. B58/177).

Piers Plowman was responsible for the association of things medieval with an aroused social conscience.[22]

The most fructifying medieval influence is the one that accounts not only for particular motifs and images or even entire poems or pages but for the very form of the composite art that is Blake's most individual and original mode of expression. No existing external evidence persuades beyond cavil that Blake was influenced by books of medieval illumination. But it is at the very least probable that the most distinguished book illuminator of modern times was intimately familiar with the medieval page, and reasonably plausible conjectures can suggest which some of those pages might have been.

Blake's illuminated books did not appear "meteor-like out of an apparent void."[23] They have as precise and relevant a context as any phenomenon of literary history. A prominent bibliophile said in 1809 that the passion for illustrated books had been violent for about a half-century.[24] Blake's early years were spent in an environment congenial to those whom Horace Walpole called "the most valuable artists" of the Middle Ages, the illuminators of manuscripts.[25]

Blake himself saw a connection between Books of Hours and his illustrated pages for he called his works "Illuminated Books." Yeats referred to the *Songs of Innocence* and *The Book of Thel* as "illuminated missals of song," and several modern scholars have detected particular resemblances in design between Blake and his medieval exemplars.[26] But more important than particular borrowings is a pervasive affinity of spirit that unites Blake with one particular epoch in illumination and perhaps also with one particular work of illuminated art.

[22] *CW*, pp. 430–31. See also *Jerusalem*, Plate 52, *CW*, pp. 681–83. In the work by Gough that Blake and his master Basire illustrated referred to above (n. 21), prominent quotations from *Piers Plowman* in black letter appear on separate pages at the head of several chapters.

[23] Review by John Harthan of the Keynes-Wolf *Census*, *The Library*, 5th ser., IX (June, 1954), 137.

[24] Thomas Frognall Dibdin, *The Bibliomania* (London, 1809), p. 61.

[25] Quoted in Gough, *op. cit.* (n. 21), Vol. II, Part I, p. 1.

[26] *CW*, p. 208; W. B. Yeats (ed.), *The Poems of William Blake* (London, 1893), p. xxxi; Anthony Blunt, "Blake's Pictorial Imagination," *Journal of the Warburg and Courtauld Institutes*, VI (1943), esp. pp. 198–200; *idem, op. cit.* (n. 9), Plate 16a—a striking juxtaposition of the "Introduction" to *Innocence* and a thirteenth-century page.

Because Blake was an illuminator acquainted with the conventions of his art, it is not surprising that occasional resemblances exist between his work and illuminated manuscripts of almost all periods, from the earliest extant papyrus manuscript of about 165 B.C. through the fourteenth century. Anticipations of Blake seem to increase as one moves later in time: fourteenth-century pages provide striking similarities in delicate sprays of leaf, flower, and fruit, in miniatures gracefully poised in initial letters, in the illustrations that divide the page at the middle, in side borders that shoot out horizontal lines to make top and bottom borders. But these resemblances are fortuitous compared to the profounder affinities that unite the opulent and animated style of fifteenth-century French illumination and the pages of *Innocence* and *Experience*, particularly in their later, heightened coloring.

Blake must surely have known particular works of late illumination. In 1786, two years before Blake's first works of reliefengraving appeared, James Edwards, a wealthy bookseller, purchased for £213 from the Duchess of Portland what is now one of the greatest treasures of the British Museum, the Bedford Hours, created by French or Flemish artists between 1430 and 1450. James Edwards was the brother of Richard Edwards, who commissioned Blake's drawings to Young and published engravings from some of them. He was the friend of Joseph Johnson, Blake's friend and early publisher, with whom Edwards stayed on first coming to London from Halifax. He is reported to have invited, during the 1780's, scholars, students, and persons of taste to examine his books, manuscripts, and missals. It is not a wild conjecture that young William Blake was one of those invited. If so, he saw the splendid Book of Hours that was its owner's proudest possession, along with Greek vases, books of engravings, incunabula printed on vellum, and other illuminated manuscripts. Of all these, it was in all likelihood the Bedford Hours that impressed the young man most, since he was looking for a medium congenial to his twin talents as painter and poet and appropriate to his experience as a maker of embellished books.[27]

[27] On James Edwards, see T. W. Hanson, "Richard Edwards, Publisher," *Times Literary Supplement*, August 8, 1942, p. 396; T. W. Hanson, "'Edwards of Halifax.' A Family of Booksellers, Collectors and Book-Binders," *Papers, Reports, &c. Read before the Halifax Antiquarian Society* (1912 [I owe this reference to Professor G. E.

Fastidious modern taste may run to the *Très riches heures* of the Duc de Berry and find the Bedford Hours to be excessive in ornament and even a bit decadent. But to Blake's young eyes, seeking fresh visual experience and learning to look for it in medieval sources, the sight of the Bedford Hours would have—to speak like a Rossetti—opened a window upon paradise. The panorama of color—from the delicate shades so similar to the earliest copies of *Innocence* to the deep blues, purples, and golds that Blake used in later coloring—would have joined with the animated forms to suggest how still another artistic world could be made. Blake's line is more fluid and eccentric, and bolder in its movement, than that of the medieval artist; but the linear motion the earlier artist achieved within rigid patterns must have been admired. In fact, the intertwining of flower, leaf, bird, tree, and human figure in the *guilloche* that borders Blake's lovely "Introduction" to *Innocence* stands indisputably in the tradition of illumination. There are also many striking anticipations of particular Blakean strokes. The blue sky with golden stars and the brooding crucifixion scene in striking blue monochrome look like Blake's Urizenic blue. The sophisticated full-page illustrations (Plates XII, XIII) giving the theme of the section that follows and using a complicated chronological and conceptual scheme of related panels are not unlike Blake's separate plates and their relation to the text that follows them. Snakes entwine the trunks of trees and encircle architectural columns, as in *Innocence, Experience,* and the illustrations to Milton; sheep, as in

---

Bentley, Jr., who kindly supplied me with the essential information it contains]); *D.N.B.; Gentleman's Magazine,* LXXXVI (1816), Part I, p. 92; Dibdin, *op. cit.* (n. 24), pp. 14 ff. On contemporary knowledge of the Bedford Hours, see Thomas Frognall Dibdin, *The Bibliographical Decameron* (London, 1817), I, cxxxviii and n.; *A Catalogue of the Valuable Library of James Edwards, Esq.* (London, 1815), item no. 830 (I have examined the Edwards catalogues of 1789, 1794, 1796, and 1815 [the last with notes by Madden] at the British Museum, and the 1790 catalogue, with notes by Douce, at the Bodleian); *An Account of a Rich Illuminated Missal Executed for John Duke of Bedford . . .* (London, 1794 [Gough's copy, containing several inserted color-copies of pages of the Bedford Missal, is at the Bodleian]). For more recent comment on the Hours, see David Diringer, *The Illuminated Book* (London, 1958), p. 404; Erwin Panofsky, *Early Netherlandish Painting* (Cambridge, Mass., 1953), I, 384 n. 3; *Illuminated Manuscripts in the British Museum* (London, 1903), Plate 5; Gustave Friedrich Waagen, *Galleries and Cabinets of Art in Great Britain* (London, 1857), pp. 21–22; *idem, Treasures of Art in Great Britain* (London, 1854), I, 127 ff.

"The Lamb" and elsewhere, huddle together in the landscape (Plate XIVA); skeletons rise from the ground, as in the Blair illustrations; devils claw at human flesh with iron hooks, as in Blake's Dante (Plate XIVB); small nude figures climb border branches, as in Blake everywhere (Plate XIII); angels blowing trumpets cross their wings near the tip, as in *Job* and *Young* (Plate XIVC); and a River of Death flows between blasted trees, as in Blake's similar, though antithetical, "River of Life"[28] (Plates XIV D, XV).

None of these can be claimed as an incontrovertible source. Raphael's Loggie design, not the Bedford Hours, may have suggested the intimacy of God and man that in *Job* brings the sufferer and his creator so close together in appearance and position. But as a totality the Bedford Hours, or a book very much like it, must be considered a very close analogue to what Blake has done. It is difficult to think of any other work or kind of work that, in the manner of Blake, combines color with linear movement, symbolic richness with naïve emblematic meaning, childlike instructiveness with mystical resonance, textual illustration with full-page renditions of biblical and Christian myth and doctrine. In the Bedford Hours the freshness of natural life unites with central human concerns; men and animals confront one another on leafy, flowery border; and beauty and horror, innocence and experience, meet in a richness of color and line that text and picture in combination were not to achieve again until William Blake created a composite style that he called "more ornamental, uniform, and grand"[29] than any ever before discovered.

[28] British Museum Add. MS 18850, esp. leaves 14r, 56r, 80v, 88v, 132r, 157r, 191r, 208r, 229v.
[29] *CW*, p. 207.

CHAPTER III

Ideal Art and the High Renaissance

Of the three adjectives Blake himself applied to his composite art
—"ornamental, uniform, and grand"[1]—*ornamental* best describes
those qualities that most resemble medieval illumination and *grand*
those that were derived from the painters and engravers of the
high Renaissance. The Gothic page inspired Blake to adorn his
literary text with color, borders, and linear motion. But the pictorial
masters of the fifteenth and sixteenth centuries, even though they
contributed heavily to Blake's form, primarily nourished his
"intellectual" being.

BLAKE'S PANTHEON

Almost every artist in the late eighteenth century produced his
own version of the sublime. Blake's friend Barry, a painter of
monumental canvases in the spirit of the *gusto grande*, rejected from
his notion of the sublime those very works—the Eddas, the Old
Testament prophecies, and the Book of Revelation, which he found
to be "barbarous, disorderly, and . . . Gothic"[2]—that were the
main constituents of Blake's sublimity, the very pillars of his
pantheon.

Blake found natural art and ideal art deeply incompatible. He
was not always content that "Historical Designing" and "Portrait
Painting" were "as Distinct as any two Arts can be," and he once
exclaimed, "Happy would that Man be who could unite them!"
But distinct they surely were, as distinct as landscape and history—
a conventional neoclassical antithesis in which Blake fully acquiesced.

It is of course a mistake to think that Blake disliked nature. He
found Felpham idyllic, loved the English seacoast and English

[1] *CW*, p. 207.
[2] Anthony Blunt, *The Art of William Blake* (New York, 1959), p. 14.

flowers and birds, and occasionally wrote nature poetry as lovely as anything the Romantics can show. But his spirit had its roots in ideal art, to which nature was often a formidable obstacle; "... if you have Nature before you at all, you cannot Paint History; it was Michael Angelo's opinion & is Mine." In old age Blake looked upon death as "Leaving the Delusive Goddess Nature & her Laws to get into Freedom from all Law of the Members into The Mind, in which every one is King & Priest in his own House." What the aged artist expected death to accomplish he had earlier expected art to accomplish: to release men from bondage to nature and from the art and science that fed on nature alone—from picturesque landscape, from Venetian color, from Newtonian mechanics, from Lockean psychology, and from fashionable portraiture. Raphael, Michelangelo, and Dürer, the main begetters of the grand style, Blake regarded as the most effectual instruments of that release.[3]

Blake borrowed more widely than one would expect, for he was not of Sir Joshua's opinion that to borrow was to flatter by imitation or emulation. Major and minor art of all epochs and work that cannot even be called art at all contributed to Blake's larder. Salviati's *Saul* may have suggested the powerful contrapposto of "My Son, My Son" in *The Gates of Paradise*. Annibale Carracci, whom apparently Blake despised as the connoisseurs' favorite and whom he regarded as his inferior even in technique, may have influenced the "Death of the Strong Wicked Man" in the Blair illustrations. The hideous figure of Death in Baccio Bandinelli's skeletons resembles some of Blake's illustrations to Young, and a drawing by or after Daniele da Volterra may be responsible for the posture of Eve in the illustration of Milton, "Adam and Eve Sleeping." An anatomical figure illustrating proportion in Scamozzi's work on architecture is a likely candidate for the source of one of Blake's most famous paintings and engravings, "Glad Day." The snaky corkscrew line that appears in *America* and elsewhere seems to have been anticipated by Luca Penni, and Blake's vegetating figures in *Jerusalem* recall the woman who is becoming a tree in Andrea Mantegna's Louvre canvas. Blake now and then recalls Tintoretto, Masaccio, Salvator Rosa, Piero della Francesca,

[3] Letters to Butts, September 11, 1801, and November 22, 1802, *CW*, pp. 810, 815; Letter to Cumberland, April 12, 1827, *CW*, p. 879; *CW*, pp. 562, 585.

35

and Andrea Orcagna, at least two of whom he may have despised. The boy who bought engravings and drawings at Langford's, Christie's, and other auction rooms early stored his mind with voluminous and lasting visual impressions upon which he drew during a long and productive life.[4]

Because his artistic borrowing is so exuberant, Blake has been accused of not having a steady aim.[5] But his objective was to transform what he borrowed to his own purpose, not to flatter or imitate the source. And his profoundest admirations never wavered from their steady direction toward three or four of the greatest masters of the European Renaissance. To these masters, though he regularly raided them for visual motifs, he turned for profounder reasons than to seize here and there an iconographical detail. They were his *almae matres*, and from them he drew the spirit and the structure of his prophetic art. Out of Dürer he quarried his emblematic and intellectual landscape, out of Michelangelo and Raphael the gigantic characters of his apocalyptic drama, and out of Giulio Romano and the chiaroscuro colorists some of his firmest symbols and actions.

So sharp is Blake's divergence from the contemporary picturesque and from romantic naturalism that his devotion to the Renaissance masters may, ironically, seem to resemble the taste of the eighteenth-century connoisseur and virtuoso. Like his neoclassical and baroque predecessors, Blake enshrined Raphael at the center of his pantheon; preferred line to color ("Venetian & Flemish Ooze")[6] and Florence to Venice; disliked the Dutch—"those drudging Mimicks [in Horace Walpole's words] of Nature's most uncomely coarseness"[7]; and rated history painting as the epic of the visual arts.

The similarities between Blake's taste and that of the academy are, however, more accidental than purposive. He was in fact a revisionist, in open war with official dogma. Blake's culture-hero Michelangelo had until recently seldom been admired without

---

[4] Blunt, *op. cit.* (n. 2), pp. 31–32, 37–38, 10, 34; Malkin's *Memoirs* in Arthur Symons, *Blake* (London, 1907), p. 313; C. H. Collins Baker, "The Sources of Blake's Pictorial Expression," *Huntington Library Quarterly*, IV (April, 1941), 359–67; Mona Wilson, *The Life of William Blake* (London, 1948), p. 219.

[5] Basil de Selincourt, *William Blake* (London, 1909), p. 23.

[6] *CW*, p. 547.

[7] *Aedes Walpolianae; or, a Description of the Collection of Pictures at Houghton-Hall in Norfolk* (2d ed., London, 1752), p. xi.

qualification in the ruling artistic circles, and the poet regarded it as an outrage that that "Dutch-English bore," Sir Joshua Reynolds, should have deified the Italian.

> 'Tis the trading English Venetian cant
> To speak Michael Angelo & Act Rembrandt.[8]

Dürer was conceded by official taste to be a genius but with serious reservations about his dry Gothic manner and his grotesque departures from classic decorum. Established notions of art history were sharply divergent from Blake's. Raphael, Correggio, Guido Reni, and Annibale Carracci—this was the apostolic succession to the age of baroque and rococo. But the last three names Blake anathematized, and he must have regarded their canonization by the academicians as blasphemous—as the degradation of Raphael's sublime to the ogee-curves of the fashionable drawing room. The virtuosi and Blake agreed about Rubens, but for different reasons. *They* distrusted his anatomical distortions and the exuberance of his allegory, while Blake hated his involvement in a corrupt society. "Statesman & a Saint," he was too much the friend of kings and queens, too much the painter of sumptuous dresses and lavish interiors.

> Rubens thinks Tables, Chairs & Stools are Grand
> But Rafael thinks A Head, a foot, a hand.[9]

What shape do Blake's admirations assume? Amazingly, they resemble what modern scholars would call "mannerist" taste. Mannerism, an anti-classical style that bridged the high Renaissance and the baroque and that expressed imaginative ideas unauthorized by nature, looked for inspiration to the Michelangelo of the "Last Judgment" and of the frescoes of the Capella Paolina, to the intellectual Raphael and the violent Giulio Romano, and to Albrecht Dürer, whose eccentricities had lost him the support of baroque-rococo aesthetics. Blake may never have consciously admired Pontormo, Rosso Fiorentino, and Parmigianino; but in striking ways his enthusiasms parallel theirs. Consciously or not, he built his pantheon according to their blueprint.

[8] *CW*, p. 542.
[9] *CW*, pp. 546, 547.

DÜRER AND MICHELANGELO

Dürer's masterpieces of copper and woodcut engraving constantly make one think of Blake. Blake's horrific Nebuchadnezzar, a human animal on all fours, looks like Dürer's "The Penance of St. John Chrysostom," in which the saint crawls in the landscape to the left, his beard flowing, his hair ropy in the manner of Blake's man-beast[10] (Plate XVI; see Plate LIB). Dürer's influence goes beyond the gift of particular themes to a pervasive tutelage of Blake's spirit. If the *Job* engravings constitute the grandest work on copper since Dürer,[11] Dürer himself deserves much of the credit.[12] His wonderfully clean line-incisions, that could express contrasts later thought possible only to paint and stipple, fully vindicated Blake's passionate support of line over tonal art. Dürer was an artist close to the written word, to the verbal concept and conceit. Sometimes the word appeared in Latin as a text or epigraph on the page opposite the engraving (in the two famous woodcut Passions, for example), and contributed the historical setting, the narrative, the unifying image, or the dramatic speech. More often, the word was only implied, but even then a biblical or mythological relevance was present and the visual scene alone, as has been amply shown, was itself capable of implying the whole intellectual structure of the Renaissance.

In the art of emblematic landscape Dürer must have been Blake's chief master. His formula for landscape—rock, serpentine tree, cave, distant scene as though in a frame, blasted trunks, gnarled branches, clouds that resemble smoke and smoke that resembles clouds, visible roots, animals in thick leaves, caverns under trees— is an astonishing anticipation of Blake's. Both men's landscapes are a visualization of the lost paradise, of nature under a curse, with

---

[10] See also Blake's color print, *Nebuchadnezzar*, in the Tate Gallery. For other uses of the same theme of the animalized man crawling on all fours, see Lucas Cranach (British Museum, Department of Prints and Drawings, B VII. 276, 1) and Hans Sebald Beham (B VIII. 208, 215). See also Cranach's *The Werewolf* (C.D. II. 310, 89), discussed by Anthony Blunt, "Blake's Pictorial Imagination," *Journal of the Warburg and Courtauld Institutes*, VI (1943), 203–4.

[11] Laurence Binyon, *The Engraved Designs of Blake* (London, 1926), p. 7.

[12] For Blake's admiration of Dürer, see Symons, *op. cit.* (n. 4), p. 362; Gilchrist, *Life* (London, 1945), pp. 302 ff; Annotations to Reynolds, *CW*, p. 461; Chaucer Prospectus, *CW*, pp. 586; and Public Address, *CW*, pp. 592, 594.

now and then a recollection of past glory and an anticipation of apocalyptic splendors to come.

Dürer's faces and figures, allegorical and realistic, may here and there have influenced Blake's *dramatis personae*. Annas, with long beard and the eye of a hypocrite, suggests a Blakean religious tyrant, and the fierce lean priest and the complacent fat one that attend Christ's circumcision make a satirical point most congenial to the creator of Urizen.[13] But in contributing characters to Blake's gallery of mythic persons and heroes, Dürer was overshadowed by Michelangelo. Fuseli came close to Blake's view when he found grandeur stamped on all Michelangelo's figures: "...his women are moulds of generation; his infants teem with the man; his men are a race of giants."[14]

Two examples show how Blake adopted the heroes of his mentor. In 1773, when he was sixteen years old, Blake engraved a giant inspired by a figure of Michelangelo. Later, having rubbed down the early plate, he redrew the giant, adding intensity to the design and interpreting its meaning by an engraved title and motto. The figure, a bearded, brooding hero, stands on a rocky coast as the sun rises (or sets) on the waters, with one foot advanced, his arms folded, his eyes cast downward. He is now identified as "Joseph of Arimathea among the Rocks of Albion"—"One of the Gothic Artists who Built the Cathedrals in what we call the Dark Ages Wandering around in sheep skins & goat skins of whom the World was not worthy such were the Christians in all ages." Michelangelo's giant has now entered Blake's myth as one of the Christian-Gothic-English heroes whom the Urizenic dispensation has driven out and on whose return the revival of culture most assuredly depends.[15]

The other example comes from Adam Ghisi's engraving after

[13] *Passio Christi* (The "Small Passion" [Nuremberg, 1511], Plate B v); *Epitome in Divae Parthenices Mariae Historiam* (Nuremberg, 1511), Plates Aiiii, Biii.

[14] Lecture II before the Royal Academy (1801), *Lectures on Painting, by the Royal Academicians. Barry, Opie, and Fuseli*, ed. Ralph N. Wornum (London, 1848), p. 382. Fuseli said of Blake that he possessed "great powers; his pencil [is] imbued with the fiery genius and bold correctness of a *Michael Angelo*" ([Blair], *The Grave, a Poem Illustrated by twelve Etchings Executed by Louis Schiavonetti, From the Original Inventions of William Blake* [London, 1808]).

[15] Geoffrey Keynes, *Blake Studies* (London, 1949), pp. 45–46 and Plate XIV.

Michelangelo of a figure from the Sistine ceiling—a young man seated on a stone, gazing at the spectator, and holding a clasped book or scroll between powerful legs (Plate XVIIA). That figure—along with others engraved by the Ghisis, from the frescoes of the Sistine Chapel—Blake copied in watercolor, slightly heightening the poetical-mystical quality of the gaze and emphasizing the extended left foot but otherwise almost exactly following the engraver (Plate XVIIB).[16] The most revealing touch by Blake is the motto he added in his own hand: "The Reposing Traveller." Once more a figure by Michelangelo has been transformed; for the motto invokes Blake's Poet, the Mental Traveller, who strides across the landscape, sometimes as a boy, sometimes as a young man, or sits under a tree or writes in a book—a Pilgrim of Eternity often driven to either flight or melancholy retirement by Urizenic society.

An early sketch in oil on paper—signed by Blake in 1776 and now at the Huntington Library—imitated a figure from the "Last Judgment." Blake seems to have returned to Michelangelo's painting for such details as the long trumpet he uses in the Blair illustrations, for such figures as the giant wrapped with a serpent who falls to the abyss on a page in *The Book of Urizen*, and for the very form of such apocalyptic masterpieces as the "Cycle of Life" in the Victoria and Albert Museum and the several versions of his own "Last Judgment."

But it is the Sistine ceiling that makes the greatest contribution. From it, more than from any other source, more even than from the poetry of Milton, Blake drew his mythic heroes. The sibyls who sit on stone slabs, God who reaches out to touch Adam, Joel who reads a scroll and Daniel who writes in a book (Plate XVIII), the lunette that contains the figure of Abias, the grieving pose of Jeremiah—all these anticipate Blake's Triple Hecate, Urizen, Los, Albion, Newton. Back of Blake's Eternals stand the powerful, noble, and gloomy giants of Michelangelo, not now in action but capable, once they move, of destroying and rebuilding a world.

[16] Blake's circle seems to have been fond of this same figure, who appears as Pericles in Fuseli's illustration of *Pericles*, V. i (see Plate XVII C), and as a prominent occupant of Hades in Flaxman's "Hermes conducting the Shades of the Suitors to Hades" (reproduced in Hans Sedlmayr, *Art in Crisis* (London, 1957), Plate 26, between pages 108 and 109).

Like their progeny, they recline on their plinths unaccompanied by picturesque decor and even without iconographical sign. Blake was to put these Eternals to work in a cosmic action of destruction and construction. But he also presents them in the darkness before dawn, when they have not as yet lost the expression Michelangelo gave them—a kind of godlike gloom amid the barren stones.

RAPHAEL AND GIULIO ROMANO

In assigning to Raphael one of the most exalted positions in his pantheon, Blake followed a persistent tradition of Western culture, one already several centuries old when the Romantic artist described the Prince of Painters as "Sublime, Majestic, Graceful, Wise."[17] Like his contemporaries and predecessors, Blake admired Raphael for the purity of his outline, for his ability to express the passions, for his subordination of natural to human values, and for the intellectuality of his most ambitious canvases. But where the orthodox saw generalized, ideal beauty, Blake saw an imaginative ability to penetrate to the mystical sublime. Raphael spread before the visionary a gallery of heroic-mythic characters in a grand and emblematic landscape. In other words, Raphael's influence was a variant of Michelangelo's and Albrecht Dürer's.

Blake seems to have been but little affected by what today we consider the quintessential Raphael, the painter of Madonnas. (Those lovely formal triumphs Blake could have seen in brilliant engravings of the Italian schools—"La Vierge à la longue cuisse," for example, one of Raimondi's most beautiful line engravings.) Nor does that Keatsian masterpiece, Raphael's "Psyche and Cupid," engraved in 1693, contain many anticipations of Blake, even though so alluring a presentation of love the author of *The Book of Thel* and the *Songs of Innocence* must have found appealing. The *Stanze* were closer to Blake's artistic purposes, and there are figures in the "Transfiguration," Raphael's most admired single canvas—Moses and Elijah, with their hair blown in the wind, their feet treading the

[17] *CW*, p. 547. See also Annotations to Reynolds, *passim*. For eighteenth- and nineteenth-century adulation of Raphael, see Jean H. Hagstrum, *The Sister Arts* (Chicago, 1958), pp. 164–65; Benjamin Ralph, *The School of Raphael* (London, n.d.); Lambert Hermanson Ten Kate, *Ideal Beauty ... Illustrated by the Works of Raphael ...* (London, 1769).

air, and Christ, "ecstatically suspended in the air"[18]—that anticipate Blake. Raphael's Cartoons—that peculiarly English treasure, now at the Victoria and Albert Museum—are also Blake-like: in sized color on paper, giving the effect of deep watercolor, they illustrate not so much the biblical story as biblical ideas. As in Blake, men and buildings predominate over sky and sea, line and form over color, light, and shade.

But none of these masterpieces competes with the designs for the Vatican Loggie, which reached a popular as well as sophisticated audience and were known as Raphael's Bible.[19] It is especially here that Raphael joins Milton and the Book of Genesis to become a major influence on Blake. The Loggie ceiling and column designs include decorative border motifs, and not since the medieval book was there so rich an anticipation of Blake's illumination as in those designs, where birds perch on snakes or fill medallions, where animals climb up the border vegetation, where birds and nude children reach for grapes, and where snakes curl around the branches. These decorations—complex, but animated, sometimes natural, more often emblematic and traditional—must have been highly suggestive to one of Blake's mental cast.

But Raphael came closest of all to anticipating Blake in his representations of the God and the men of Genesis. Blake's Milton illustration of Adam and Eve partaking of the fruit resembles Raphael's beautiful and rare scene. The similarities in Raphael between God and Noah (Plate XIXA) and between God and Abraham anticipate the resemblance of Job and his God in the Blake engravings (Plate LXXVII). The discs that represent Joseph's dream look like the disc that represents the past of Paola and Francesca in the Dante series and resemble the *mandorla* in which Los sees his vision of Jerusalem (*Jerusalem*, Plate 14). Isaac, who kneels to a Blakean God flying close to the ground (Plate XIXB), is himself Blake's Mental Traveller, who also carries a staff; and the

[18] Benito Pardo di Figueroa, *An Analysis of the Picture of the Transfiguration by Raffaello* ... (London, 1817), p. 1.

[19] *Sacrae Historiae Actae a Raphaele* ... (Rome, 1649); *Imagines Veteris ac Novi Testamenti a Raphaele* ... *in Vaticani Palatii* ... (Rome, 1674); *The New Testament Adapted to the Capacities of Children* (with designs by Raphael) (London, 1755); *Loggie di Rafaele nel Vaticano* (1772, 1776); *The Protestant's Family Bible* (London, 1780), with illustrations by Raphael, one of which (plate for Gen. 18:2) was engraved by Blake.

God of the Annunciation, who holds a globe and raises two fingers in blessing, is another Blakean deity. The God who floats through space, as beard and mantle flow in the air, is on the way to becoming Blake's Jehovah-Urizen.[20] And the creating God who in one scene (Plate XX) divides light from darkness, literally pushing back the two antithetical elements, and who in another (Plate XXII) creates the sun with his left hand and the moon with his right, provided Blake with one of the most frequently repeated visual motifs of the prophetic books. On the title page of *Milton* (Plate XXIV) the nude poet is given the posture and gesture of Raphael's God, and in *The Book of Urizen* Los, a nude figure with streaming hair, pushes two clouds or mountains apart with his extended arms while Urizen begins his journey through his creation by pushing a globe of fire against the firmament (Plates XXI, XXIII). Stothard painted and designed a frontispiece to a work by Priestley on philosophy, in which a scantily clad personification pushes one cloud with her right hand and another with her left and illustrates the title, "Philosophy dispersing the Clouds from the Garden of Science."[21] There was precedent for using Raphael's visualization of divine creation to illustrate late eighteenth-century thought.

Giulio Romano, the pupil of Raphael, had been so intimately associated with his master on the Loggie designs that modern scholarship does not agree about the role to assign each artist. Even so, Giulio's influence on Blake was no mere repetition of Raphael's. Blake's eyes, which saw a sublimely heroic Raphael, saw also a sublimely terrible Romano—the creator of the grandiose, menacing, catastrophic frescoes of the Palazzo del T in Mantua, a work that a modern scholar has called "the most fantastic and frightening creation of the entire Italian Renaissance in any medium."[22] In superb engravings of this masterpiece[23] Blake saw the mouths of

[20] These illustrations of the Bible may be consulted in *Works of Raffaelle, Domenichino, Poussin, and Albano* (London, 1819), the first two volumes of which are devoted to Raphael.

[21] Engraved by William Sharp. See Huntington Library collection of engravings, Print Box 785.

[22] Frederick Hartt, *Giulio Romano* (New Haven, 1958), I, 153.

[23] See esp. the engravings after Romano by the Ghisis in the British Museum, Department of Prints and Drawings (Separate Portfolio C62*). Blake rated Romano's masterpiece far above Rubens' Luxembourg Gallery, which he called the work of a blockhead; in it "Bloated Gods ... & the rattle traps of Mythology & the lumber of an awkward French Palace are thrown together around Clumsy and Ricketty Princes &

male and female giants opened in the horror of the Greek tragic mask; he saw giants among rocks, temples crumbling, the mixing of men, mules, goats, and satyrs in mythic action. He saw monstrous fish, the hideous battles of predatory animals, brooding allegorical figures with Roman profiles writing on tablets, and mythic men and women and biblical heroes placed in the rocky allegorical landscape, where roots expose themselves above the eye-level of the human characters (Plate XXV). In Romano, Blake encountered a genius who, like himself, was able to place the heroes of Michelangelo and Raphael in the allegorical landscape of Dürer and to create for them actions of great originality and power.

The motifs of the Mantuan artist seem to have been peculiarly capable of being transformed by a revolutionary like Blake into social and mythic meaning. Romano's prisoners, each chained and tortured in a different way, must have seized the attention of an artist who so often represents the prisoner's cave and chain. The coat of hamated mail, resembling the scales of a fish (as in the famous painting "The Accusers of Theft, Adultery, and Murder"[24]) that Blake made stand for war and violence, for oppressive moral-classical "virtue," and for political and social tyranny, could have had a thousand sources (see Plate LXVIA). It may have been suggested by Milton's Sin, whose body is a woman's to the waist but ends "foul in many a scaly fould" (*Paradise Lost*, II, 653), or by the engraved title page of Drayton's *Poly-Olbion* of 1622, on which one of the several conquerors of Britain appears wearing the scaly mailed vest. But is there, in the work of any artist Blake may have known, so striking and obsessive a use of scaly armor as in Giulio Romano's "Triumph of the Emperor Sigismund"[25] (Plate XXVI)? In this military procession men wear the dress of war, and their faces show anger or fear. Ostensibly, we have a visual description—along with the interpretative words of the art-critic

Princesses higgledy piggledy. On the Contrary, Juilio Romano's Palace of T at Mantua is allow'd on all hands to be the Production of a Man of the Most Profound sense & Genius . . . " (Public Address, *c.* 1810, *CW*, p. 599). I owe the reading "Production," instead of "Product," to Mr. Erdman.

[24] Binyon, *op. cit.* (n. 11), Plate X.

[25] Engraved by de Rubeis under the title *Sigismundi Augusti Mantuam Adeuntis Prefectio Triumphus . . .* (Rome, 1680). The originals were done in 1529–30, to celebrate one of the visits of the Emperor Charles V (Hartt, *op. cit.* [n. 22], I, 148). Blake has Tharmas wear "scaly armour" in *Vala, or the Four Zoas* I, 186 (*CW*, p. 269).

Bellori—of a mighty imperial army. But the combination of a military detail, like the scaly armored vests, with fierce, diabolical, and inhuman faces must have been regarded by Blake as being a powerful satirical commentary. To his eyes the procession could not have been viewed calmly as a neutral historical document. He must have seen in it grimly militarized men, women, and boys, from whom tyranny had exacted the price of their humanity.

ENGRAVED MASTERPIECES

It has been lamented that Blake and his contemporaries were usually denied the sight of high Renaissance masterpieces in their original color and were doomed to view them in the black and white of popular engraving. We need not be so patronizing about an art that Dürer had used to duplicate the work of his own pencil, that added the skill of Marcantonio Raimondi, the Ghisis, or Agostino Veneziano to the genius of Raphael, Michelangelo, or Giulio Romano, and that had received the sponsorship of Raphael, himself impressed by the example of Albrecht Dürer. Blake regarded engraving as capable of vigorous and economical statement, an art that must have reinforced, if it did not create, his strong prejudice against Venetian color and his equally strong partiality to Florentine and Roman line. Looking at the mass of engraved art that was Blake's heritage, one gets no sense of limitation or loss. Aldegrever, Lucas van Leyden, Bonasone, the Sadelers and many others are masters of a form of literary-intellectual communication that does not require apology and that, both in its duplication of Renaissance masterpieces and in its own original creations, constitutes one of the most important influences upon his own poetic-pictorial art. The art of the engraver was never far from the literary text which had inspired it and to which, in profoundly philosophical ways, it was related. Even when words do not appear on the plate, engravings of the type Blake admired were always rooted in words and concepts.

Out of the main tradition of copper and wood engraving there arose a technique of producing color, light, and shade by successive printings on slightly colored paper from three wood blocks exactly the same in size. The first furnished the outlines and the pen hatchings, the second the highlights and the less powerful shadows, the third the stronger shadows. These chiaroscuro woodcuts— "a very beautiful and ingenious invention," in the words of Vasari, who attributed it to Ugo da Carpi[26]—soon acquired unique characteristics that lasted through the work of LeSueur in the eighteenth century. In its heyday during the sixteenth and seventeenth centuries it produced mannerist adaptations of high Renaissance art that stressed violent action in "sympathetic" landscapes. Without destroying the essential features of the tradition of Dürer, Michelangelo, Raphael, and Giulio, it added individual eccentricities of form and function. Without ever becoming picturesquely tonal, without ever weakening the constituent lines, its colors and its chiaroscuro added depth, emotional resonance, and melodramatic action to the familiar biblical and pagan allegories.

This art, particularly as it was practiced by its founder Ugo da Carpi, who lived in the sixteenth century, and by Hendrick Goltzius, who died in 1598, has many parallels, not to the Blake of *Innocence* and *Experience*, which recall illuminated Books of Hours, but to the Blake of *America*, *Urizen*, *Europe*, *Jerusalem*, and *Milton*—the Blake of the major and minor prophecies. The green, blue, or sepia paper and ink are reduplicated in Blake's use of colored ink for text and design. Some of the figures, like Ugo's Diogenes or like Goltzius's Sun God (Plate XXVIIB), Hercules, or Tantalus (Plate XXVIIIA), look ahead to Blake's prophetic giants (Plate XXVIIIB) and natural personifications (Plate XXVIJA). Such a persistent motif as Blake's looping line reminds one of Goltzius's often repeated squiggle; and a typical Goltzius scene, in which the Goddess of the Night rides on a cart pulled by bats, anticipates eminently Blakean devices and motifs. No one can say for certain that typical chiaroscuro representations—a man enclosed in a gloomy cave writing on tablets (Plate XXIX)—directly stimulated Blake. But the mannerist distortion and emotion that one sees in the chiaroscuros of Ugo and Goltzius do resemble important features of Blake's prophetic world.[27]

[26] *The Lives of the Painters Sculptors and Architects* ("Everyman's Library" [London, 1950]), II, 238.

[27] Particularly in the dark bodies with white highlights in some versions of *Milton* and *Jerusalem*. Blake mentions Goltzius with Dürer (*Public Address, c.* 1810, *CW,* p. 594). Goltzius and Ugo were known to Blake's contemporaries. See William Young Ottley, *A Collection of Fac-Similes of Scarce and Curious Prints* (London, 1826), I, xxv; Matthew Pilkington, *A Dictionary of Painters* (London, 1805), p. 226. Blake's scornful comments on chiaroscuro (*CW,* p. 554) do not apply to the engravers here discussed but to Venetian artists and their English followers, who underrated outline and who strove for "one Generalizing Tone."

Mannerist engraving in color may have been a more important influence on Blake than has been known or than can now be proved. But it should not be regarded alone, out of the context in which we have considered it. Blake doubtless saw it for what it was, a powerful and original adaptation, not a disruption, of the great tradition. For the masters of Blake—Raphael, Michelangelo, and Dürer—were also the masters of the chiaroscuro engravers. And the earlier artists—especially, as Blake saw them, in the powerful line engravings of the seventeenth century—constituted a body of mythic and intellectual art to which his aspired as the flower does to the sun.

CHAPTER IV

The Emblem

Blake's relations with the seventeenth century were profound and complex. His coarse humor, his dissenter's idiom, his message of the "Everlasting Gospel" may have been indebted to the religious-revolutionary tradition of the Ranters, those most uncompromising of the English antinomians.[1] John Milton's poems, next to the Bible—indeed, as an adjunct to the Bible—were the most formative literary and spiritual influence on the author of *Milton* and the illustrator of almost all the poems from the *Nativity Ode* to *Paradise Regained*. But to the eclectic masters of Bologna, whom Blake's century adored—Guido Reni and the Carracci—Blake was either hostile or indifferent; and to a most robust and impressive tradition, baroque book illustration, which he must have preferred to the lighter and more playful rococo of his own day, he displayed only fortuitous resemblances. These—an occasional border with Blakean foliation, powerfully constructed bodies in motion, a rugged emblematic landscape—anticipate Blake only because he and these seventeenth-century illustrators had a background in common—the illuminated manuscript, Dürer and the German engravers, the mannerist side of the high Renaissance masters.[2]

With the emblem books, however, which were produced in quantity in the sixteenth century, which persisted up to the very time of Blake, but which reached a kind of culmination in the seventeenth century of the Counter-Reformation, Blake's connection is obvious and indisputable. To the emblem Blake's composite art bore a generic as well as genetic relation—a relation it bore to no other antecedent form except books of illumination. Not only do Blake's "Gates of Paradise" and "All Religions Are One" owe many details to emblems, they *are* emblems—just as the *Songs of Innocence* not only borrow motifs here and there from illuminated manuscripts but are themselves illuminations.

[1] A. L. Morton, *The Everlasting Gospel* (London, 1958).
[2] Cf. Philip Hofer, *Baroque Book Illustration* (Cambridge, Mass., 1951).

The tradition of emblematic expression, paradoxically, pulled in two opposite directions. When serving the pedagogical aims of the religious *kulturkampf* that brought Christian truth to the illiterate masses and to young learners, emblems tended to be popular, proverbial, simple, crude in execution, and concerned with the commonplaces of human experience. But when tickling the taste and vanity of aristocrats the emblem—more particularly the devices or *imprese* which appeared on private coats of arms and bookplates— was esoteric, witty, metaphysical—ambitious to embody all that a bold and learned imagination could conceive.[3] The century in which Blake came to intellectual maturity tended to reject the seventeenth-century emblem in both its vulgar and sophisticated orientations. Shaftesbury found these figures impolite and crude, "bad figures" produced by "bad minds," "crooked designs" made by "crooked fancies."[4] Barry called the emblems of Vaenius and the icons of Ripa the "offal of the imagination,"[5] and another friend, Fuseli, praised Blake's designs for Blair as eschewing Gothic and far-fetched symbols and spreading "a familiar and domestic atmosphere."[6] But Blake, ignoring the advice of his age and of his friends, made his art profoundly emblematic. Sometimes he produced simple-seeming proverbs and designs "For Children"; sometimes, gnomic aphoristic hieroglyphs "For the Sexes." Blake was fully committed to Fuseli's aphorism that "All ornament ought to be allegoric."[7]

The antecedent emblem is important less because it gave to Blake many of his visual and verbal motifs than because it helps us define and understand Blake's manner of expression. His emblems, like those of the tradition that taught him, embodied three related but separable elements: personifications, natural and artistic details allegorically intended, and original imaginative constructions.

PERSONIFICATIONS

Perhaps the most characteristic feature of Blake's style is its

[3] Cf. Jean H. Hagstrum, *The Sister Arts* (Chicago, 1958), chap. iv.
[4] *Second Characters or the Language of Forms*, ed. Benjamin Rand (Cambridge, Mass., 1914), p. 105. Shaftesbury is here referring to exotic Oriental representations, but his comments on the barbarous emblems are closely similar.
[5] *Works of James Barry* (London, 1809), I, 468.
[6] Illustrations to *The Grave* (London, 1808), p. xiv.
[7] Eudo C. Mason, *The Mind of Henry Fuseli* (London, 1951), p. 245.

original and absolutely central use of personification. That kind of language he learned immediately from his poetic predecessors in the eighteenth century and only remotely from the emblematists of the seventeenth. For, as Blake's first poems reveal, he belonged to the school of the Wartons, Thomson, Collins, and Gray, whose distinguishing stylistic quality was a picture-like organization of reality around a central personified figure. Blake's seasons in the *Poetical Sketches* resemble Thomson's and Collins's, and his mature descriptions were always governed by natural personification. But like the same literary school, notably Collins and Gray, Blake also used, with great familiarity and skill, the emblematic or allegorical personification. The creation of such figures in both painting and poetry was thought to display imaginative power at its very highest stretch.[8] Blake illustrated Young and Gray, acutely aware of how important their pictorial personifications were; he surrounds—and sometimes overwhelms—the page with figures that represent Spring, Evening, Winter, the Sun, Death, Reason, Melancholy, Conscience—figures that recall pictured myth and sculptured stone (Plates IV, XXVIIA). Blake was an *iconologist* in its eighteenth-century meaning: he practiced "the Art of personifying the Passions, Arts, Sciences, Dispositions of the Mind, Virtues, Vices &c."[9]

But Blake's adherence to Wartonian aesthetics explains only a part of his art. Had he not gone beyond that influence, he would have been an Angelica Kauffmann or an Edward Young of genius. But he would not have been the Blake who transformed Thomson's Winter into Urizen and Gray's Spring into Los; who made skeletons fly, flowers copulate, trees embrace with snaky arms; and who saw Church and State as the apocalyptic beings of a new Book of Daniel and Revelation. The personifications of the Blake we know—less smoothly conventional, more palpable, more directly the creatures of vision than the personifications of the Wartonian school—have the aura of earlier and simpler emblematic personifications about them. For Blake's figures have fed upon works produced not in the worldly eighteenth century but in an age of faith and primitive, otherworldly seeing. George Aemylius, Hans Sebald Beham, Bocchius, Jacob Cats, Alciati, Otto Vaenius, Francis Quarles,

[8] Hagstrum, *op. cit.* (n. 3), esp. pp. 270–74.

[9] George Richardson, *Iconology; or, A Collection of Emblematical Figures, Moral and Instructive* (London, 1778), I, i.

George Wither, Ripa, Paradin, and many others surely caught Blake's young eye in the engraver's shop where he worked and in the print shops he frequented as a boy (Plate XXX). They have left their mark in the pleasing and persuasive naïveté of the Blakean figure.

NATURE, GEOGRAPHY, AND ARCHITECTURE

Had Samuel Johnson been able to paint, he would never have reproduced vegetation, because a blade of grass was only and ever a blade of grass. But Blake, though never fashionably picturesque, did copy nature, precisely because it never remained only that in the totality of his system.

The newt and frog that swim in Blake's water, the sheep that huddle at the bottom of his page, the spider that threads his web from the upper corner, the beetle that crawls between the lines of text, the bat that flies in the border, the pebble that sings in the brook, the lion that peeps through the leaves, the sunflower that follows the sun, and the rose that falls to the ground—this rich array of natural life can be matched elsewhere in Blake's day—in handsomely produced botanical treatises,[10] say, or in the extremely popular aquatints. But it is only the ant and the bee, the spider and the scarab beetle, of the emblem—where they convey moral and mystical meanings—that provide the exact context for the natural life of Blake's pages (see Plate LXXVI). For he must have agreed with Meister Eckhart that "anything known or born is an image,"[11] an image, that is, of something else. Blake's often repeated aphorism, "All that lives is holy," meant, not that everything alive is lovely or good—consider the bat and the blood-thirsty flea—but that everything has the dignity of meaning, as well as the integrity of indestructible individuality.

Nowhere outside Blake is the serpent so prominent as in the emblem books of the sixteenth and seventeenth centuries (Plate XXXB). In the *Orus Apollo* the snake in a circle symbolizes time and eternity, and, when it bites its tail, the world; in Paradin it symbolizes,

---

[10] See Robert John Thornton, *The Temple of Flora* (London, 1801); Maria Sybilla Meriaen, *Over de Voortteeling en Wonderbaerlyke Veranderingen der Surinaamsche Insecten* (Amsterdam, 1730).

[11] Quoted by George Wingfield Digby, *Symbol and Image in William Blake* (Oxford, 1957), p. 112.

when alone, the artist's imagination, but it stands for danger when it crawls in the grass. Entwining a cross, the serpent recalls Moses' brazen serpent lifted up in the wilderness and prefigures the cross of Christ; but wound around a tree, it recalls the eating of the fatal apple in Eden (Plate XXXA). The eternity of secular love is symbolized by a snake swallowing its tail if a cupid sits in the circle formed; the eternity of divine love if the snake encloses a flame and a pitcher of water; the frustration of natural inclination by divine prudence if the snake encircles a star. Among the ancients, among the later emblematists, and even among Blake's contemporaries the serpent might symbolize envy, health, a wounded conscience, or the power of life to renew itself.[12]

Blake's natural emblems lose rhetorical force if we do not know the conventional meaning and fail to see how it has sometimes been reversed (see Plate LXVIB). In a contemporary book of icons Richardson names a woman "Inconsideration," who steps off a precipice and looks, not at where she is going, but at the butterfly in her hand while the rule and compass of prudence lie neglected on the ground.[13] Blake's use of these same details completely reverses Richardson's meanings: the butterfly symbolizes the good, imaginative, and bold person, and the compass stands for the god of this mechanical world. What Richardson condemns as inconsideration Blake praises as divine excess.

The geographical and architectural emblem does more than assemble natural or artificial objects, each of which has an agreed conventional meaning. The ensemble itself is given corporate meaning and even a personality. Cities, rivers, continents, states are personified—as in the icons of Ripa—and entire landscapes can be allegorical or symbolic. Blake's tiny woodcuts for Vergil's pastorals are not, as has been widely thought, merely picturesque—

---

[12] *Orus Apollo de Aegypte* ... (1543), pp. aii (verso), aiii (recto); Francis Quarles, *Emblemes* (London, 1635), p. 4; Claude Paradin, *Heroic Emblems* (1551), cited in Thomas Frognall Dibdin, *Bibliographical Decameron* (London, 1817), I, 268–69; Claude Paradin, *Devises Heroiques* (Lyons, 1557), p. 11; William Paradin, *Historiarum Memorabilium ex Genesi* (Lyons, 1558), emblem for n. 3; Otto Vaenius, *Amorum Emblemata* (Antwerp, 1608), p. 1; *idem, Emblemata sive Symbola a Principibus* ... *aliisque usurpanda* (Brussels, 1624), Nos. 32, 40, 43; George Wither, *A Collection of Emblemes, Ancient and Moderne* (2d ed., London, 1635), pp. 74, 102, 109, 142, 151 (1st ed., 1634); Richard Payne Knight, *The Symbolical Language of Ancient Art and Mythology* (2d ed.; New York, 1892), p. 14 (1st ed. privately printed in 1818).

[13] *Op. cit.* (n. 9), Vol. I, Plate XXXIX, Fig. 152.

the "little dells, and nooks, and corners of Paradise"[14]—but powerful moral emblems in which the blasted wheat, the agitated shepherds, the dead trunk, the darkened moon are signs of a fallen world (Plate XXXI). Such landscape emblems have their antecedents in the seventeenth century, notably in the work of the Sadelers, whom Blake admired.[15] The geographical emblem was in fact one of the most important forms of instruction in the Counter-Reformation.

The seventeenth-century map bears signs of having been produced in the Age of Emblems. The maps of John Speed,[16] accurate though they strove to be, were more than maps; they were works of composite art. Borders contained personified figures as well as decorative motifs, and on the map itself dolphins decorated the sea, zephyrs symbolized the air, allegorical figures represented the various occupations, and cities were personified by icons that embodied their traditions, values, and typical human and geographical features (Plate XXXII). Because the entire city or locality was conceived of as an entity, the artist tried to present it entire in a manner not unlike the aerial view of a modern city.

Blake was so steeped in the emblem tradition that even the geographical icon seems to have caught his fancy. His engraved landscape ("A View of Chichester") recalls the cities of the topographical emblem. The illustration for *Paradise Regained* (I. 21–28) and in *Jerusalem* (Plates 57, 92) the representations of York, London, and Jerusalem look like the miniature place-emblems of Speed (Plate XXXIII). York is represented by a tiny skyline; London, by a sketch of St. Paul's, which stands for the neoclassical Establishment; and Jerusalem, by the Gothic spires that in Blake always foretell redemption. Architectural remains, associated with the Druids and available to Blake in the researches of Stukeley and other contemporary antiquarians, contributed emblems to the

[14] Samuel Palmer, quoted in Alexander Gilchrist, *Life of William Blake* ("Everyman's Library" [London, 1945]), p. [xii].

[15] Matthew Raderus, *Bavaria Sancta* (1615); *idem, Bavaria Pia* (1628); Raphael Sadler, *Expeditionis in utramque Austriam & Bohemiam* (1621); *idem, E. Puteani Bruma* (Munich, 1619). All these works contained engravings created by members of the Sadeler family. Blake mentions "Sadeler" in connection with Dürer, Goltzius, and Edelinck (Public Address, *c.* 1810, *CW*, p. 594).

[16] *Map of America* (1626); *The Theatre of the Empire of Great Britaine* (London, 1627); *A Prospect of the Most Famous Parts of the World* (London, 1676).

prophetic books. The serpent temple at Avebury symbolized the most depraved aspects of the Urizenic dispensation—the debasement of prophetic religion to human sacrifice. And the Druidic cromlech and the Mental Traveller who takes his journey under it seem to represent the man of imagination driven to flight in a society dominated by reason.[17]

THE IMAGINATIVE EMBLEM

Some seventeenth-century emblems were as witty and complex as a conceit by Donne or Marvell; others embodied the *consensus gentium* and were, as Fuseli once said, "the verdicts of wisdom on the reports of experience."[18] Emblems that were merely witty or were designed to make traditional wisdom memorable may not at first be supposed to have appealed to a revolutionary artist in full revolt against the Establishment. But Blake believed in the common man —in the intuitive wisdom of his childhood and in his imaginative power and untrammeled instincts—and in the primordial wisdom revealed in song, ballad, and proverb. His "Death's Door" is deeply involved in the language and thought of the people (Plate VA). Traditionally associated with Christ's entering limbo—as in Mantegna's representation of Christ about to enter the dungeon of hell through the door of death now broken down[19]—the phrase was popularly used in Blake's time, as in ours, to refer to death. Lord Auchinleck wrote his son James Boswell in 1765 that he had been dangerously ill and "was at death's door."[20]

The maker of proverbial emblems looked for the visual personification that lurked behind the commonplace phrase. The maker of divine emblems searched for the visual equivalents of God, doctrine,

[17] Laurence Binyon, *The Engraved Designs of Blake*, Plate 84; Darrel Figgis, *The Paintings of Blake* (New York, 1925), Plate 23; William Stukeley, *Abury, A Temple of the British Druids* (London, 1743); Blake, *Milton*, Plate 4 (*Huntington Library copy*); *Jerusalem*, Plates 70, 100; Peter F. Fisher, "Blake and the Druids," *Journal of English and Germanic Philology*, LVIII (October, 1959), 589–612; Ruthven Todd, *Tracks in the Snow* (New York, 1947), pp. 50–56 and Plate XIV.

[18] "Advertisement," John Caspar Lavater, *Aphorisms on Man* (London, 1788), p. v.

[19] British Museum, Department of Prints and Drawings, 1874-6-13-656. For Blake's "Death's Door," see *The Gates of Paradise*, Plate 23; *America*, Plate 12; and the final plate of the Blair illustrations (*op. cit.* [n. 6]).

[20] *Boswell on the Grand Tour: Italy, Corsica, and France, 1765–1766*, ed. Frank Brady and Frederick A. Pottle (London, 1955), p. 226.

heaven, and mystical union. Vaenius used a white center, surrounded by clouds and spires of radiance, as a symbol of divine love, to illustrate the text, "Oculus non vidit, nec auris audivit." Elsewhere the Deity was represented by an egg-shaped radiance with the Hebrew letters for God in the center.[21]

Blake also used the Hebrew letters to represent God, the disc or *mandorla* to represent mystical vision, the mundane egg to represent the created universe, the last being one of the oldest symbols of the created universe: the "Notion of the Mundane Egg, or that the World was Oviform," wrote Thomas Burnet, "hath been the Sense and Language of all Antiquity, Latins, Greeks, Persians, Aegyptians, and others." As if to support his own practice, Blake praised the symbols in Law's translation of Boehme, which, he is supposed to have said, Michelangelo himself could not have surpassed.[22]

But such examples as these are not numerous, and Blake does not in fact use many mystical signs. Believing that God was man and that man was God, that we all come from One Man and will one day become One Man, Blake usually found human and natural personification adequate to his purposes. His visualizations are emblematic but seldom cabbalistic; they embody men, animals, flowers, and buildings, but not often numbers, geometrical shapes, algebraic equations, wheels, cycles, and the elaborate paraphernalia of the mystics. Blake may have been mannerist in his use of unnaturally distorted forms and in his artistic defiance of natural law, but he was not surrealist. The range of his imagery may extend from the womb—is there any artist whose shapes are more unmistakably fetal than Blake's? (Plates LIVA, LVIIA)—to the tomb; but his emblems usually arise from natural experience, however weighty the meaning they must bear. In fact, Blake's forms are freshly, naïvely appealing because they remain so insistently human even when they appear in the outer reaches of the universe and attempt to embody the invisible and unknowable.

[21] Otto Vaenius, *Amoris Divini Emblemata* (Antwerp, 1660), p. 9; Robert Whitehall (author of the Epistle to the Reader), *ΕΞΑΣΤΙΧΟΝ ΙΕΡΟΝ sive Iconum Quarunda extranearum explicatio* ... (Oxford, 1677), icon. No. 4.

[22] See *Illustrations of ... Job*, title page; "The Circle of the Lustful," in Albert S. Roe, *Illustrations to the Divine Comedy* (Princeton, 1953), Plates 10, 10 E; *Milton*, Plate 33, *CW*, p. 523; Marjorie Nicolson, *Mountain Gloom and Mountain Glory* (Ithaca, 1959), p. 78; Blake to Crabb Robinson in Arthur Symons, *Blake* (London, 1907), p. 290

One page of *Innocence*—the second of two devoted to "The Ecchoing Green" (Plate XXXV)—illustrates fully all the emblematic qualities that Blake absorbed—the direct appeal to children and beyond them to the listening adult; the presence of proverbial wisdom as a substratum; the transformation of human beings and natural details into a universal symbol. The poem, which transforms a day of childish sport and its end into a symbol of the beginning and decline of life, is accompanied by designs that reinforce and amplify the meaning. On the first page (Plate XXXIV), a boy with a hoop and a boy with a bat make more specifically and palpably human the verbal description of a summer's day. On the second page, children pick grapes from a vine that extends up the right-hand side to form a border and hand them to members of the group that now returns home from play. The action, which Blake repeated elsewhere (Plate XXXV; see also Plate XXXVII), symbolizes one of the important meanings of the poem—the passage from innocence to experience through the gate of sex.

Behind Blake's page lays centuries of analogous visualization. In a missal of 1498 a woman on the ground catches the apples thrown down by two boys in a tree[23] (Plate XXXVIB). In one of the Loggie designs of Raphael nude children climb a vine and pick clusters of grapes, a design that Giulio Romano repeated in the borders of one of his mythological actions.[24] William Lily's famous school grammar was almost regularly accompanied, from 1567 to 1768, with an illustration of boys picking, throwing, beating down, or handing fruit from a tree[25] to children below (Plate XXXVIA). The centuries-old emblem was still alive in Blake's troubled day: after Waterloo the English soldiers, remembering their schoolboy habits, stopped at every halt to invade the local fruit trees, which were loaded "like the epigrammatic tree in Lily's Grammar, only with soldiers instead of scholars"[26] (Plate XXXVIB).

[23] Printed by Verard, discussed and illustrated in Dibdin, *op. cit.* (n. 12), I, 101.

[24] *Loggie di Rafaele nel Vaticano* (Part II, 1776), 2d ser., No. 8; Giulio Romano, British Museum, Department of Prints and Drawings (separate portfolio C62*).

[25] See Vincent J. Flynn (ed.), *A Shorte Introduction of Grammar by William Lily* (New York, 1945)—a facsimile reprint of the Folger Library copy. See also Gilles Sadeler after Paul Bril—an apple-picking scene with ladders against the trees (British Museum, Department of Prints and Drawings [Case 54*]).

[26] Dibdin (*op. cit.* [n. 12], p. 101) quotes a contemporary writer named Paul (*Letters to His Kinfolk*). I owe to Professor Gerald E. Bentley, Jr., the identification of "Paul" as Sir Walter Scott.

Blake's emblem creates its deep and mysterious resonances not only because it is freshly original but also because it is profoundly traditional. The emblem glows because it closes a circuit that connects us with Lily and Raphael, the Renaissance schoolboy and the English soldier in Napoleon's France.[27]

[27] See Piloo Nanavutty, "Blake and Emblem Literature," *Journal of the Warburg and Courtauld Institutes*, XV (1952), 258–61. If the argument of the present chapter is valid, then surely Miss Raine ("Blake and Tradition," *Encounter*, VII [November, 1956], 51–54) is closer to the truth than Mr. Eliot, who finds Blake's ideas cranky and eccentric because they are outside the "framework of accepted and traditional ideas" ("Blake" [1920], in *Selected Essays, 1917–1932* [London, 1932], p. 308). But though Miss Raine's view is just—that Blake's symbols (the sea, river, cave, tree, marsh, dark valley) are truly traditional—her comment that he never does violence to their conventional meanings is not fair to his habit of adapting them to his own purposes.

CHAPTER V

Illustration: Blake and His Contemporaries

Blake began his career when neoclassical law was yielding to preromantic fashion and when the same architect was capable of building Grecian one year and Gothic the next. Such variety was reflected in the Shakespeare Gallery, to which the shrewd Alderman Boydell commissioned both leading and aspiring painters to contribute. Today we would find a project devoted exclusively to historical paintings highly restricted. Blake's contemporaries saw in Boydell's venture diversity and originality—signs of English genius, nurtured by free political institutions. Sir Joshua wrote to Burke, who had called Boydell's a "very extraordinary undertaking," that "no single school at present in Europe could produce so many good pictures, and if they did they would have a monotonous sameness: they would be all Roman or Venetian, Flemish or French: whereas you may observe here, as an emblem of the Freedom of the Country, every artist has taken a different road to what he conceives to be excellence, and many have obtained the goal."[1]

"Ah, dear Marwood, what's integrity to an opportunity?" If Lady Wishfort's brittle wit can decently be adapted to Blake and his age, one might say that his monumental integrity cannot be fully understood and admired unless it is viewed along with the opportunities his diverse and bewildering times provided. Those opportunities sometimes came as challenges—Fuseli's example clearly was. But they were also temptations—to conventionality, to easy prostitution, to fashionable success. Blake's achievement today gives us such a strong impression of having been in the fury fused— the fury of a private imagination, that is—that we forget he must

[1] Quoted by T. S. R. Boase, "Illustrations of Shakespeare's Plays in the Seventeenth and Eighteenth Centuries," *Journal of the Warburg and Courtauld Institutes*, X (1947), 96.

have been a greatly tempted man. He was of this world and, like many poor men looking for success, was more vulnerable than those with all the hereditary safeguards. Blake's age was beguiling to him precisely because it offered a variety of attractive temptations. Blake's friends and collaborators were often successful conformists, who pointed the way to quick achievement in several accepted modes. Blake won his integrity, not by ignoring the diverse opportunities that late eighteenth-century England provided, but by absorbing, testing, refining, and transcending them. The greatest debt that Blake owed his environment was that it opened so many different paths to his feet. He was not in the position of Alexander Pope, who was forced—or at least so he was made to feel—to choose the path of correctness. That in fact was about the only path that Blake's time and temperament had closed to him.

Even Blake's technical processes show the restless experimenter at work. He used watercolor and tempera, and experimented with a paint that would be superior in vivacity and durability to the traditional oils. He recommended movable frescoes to his colleagues and to the leaders of his society. He adapted to his own purpose most of the engraving media of the late eighteenth century, which was—unlike the classical period, when engravers for the most part worked in line on copper—an age of considerable experimentation. Blake was both a black-and-white engraver and an illuminator. He engraved on copper, wood, stone, and pewter, and used acid to produce, not intaglio, as was fashionable, but relief.

His practice, though experimental and varied, was always guided by consistent conviction. Although as an illustrator of others' work he used more than one medium, his forte was engraving on copper —a most significant choice since this was the method of Dürer and the great Italian masters and since its aesthetic quality was strength of line, not the easy flow of line or the depth of chiaroscuro that made needle-point etching, the mezzotint, and the aquatint so popular. Even Blake's "discovery," the use of acid to produce relief, broke with the tendencies of the times. His contemporaries used acid to soften line and heighten tone. Blake used acid to submerge tone and bring out line.

At the very end of the century (1797) there appeared a sumptuous edition of Thomson's *Seasons* embellished by the engravings of Bartolozzi and Tomkins, "Engravers to their Majesties," after originals painted for this particular work by William Hamilton—an eclectic work that reveals most of the artistic tendencies that touched Blake. The frontispiece, in which the personified seasons adorn the bust of Thomson, recalls that earlier favorite, Rubens' "Nature Adorned by the Graces." The "Argument" of "Spring" is decorated in eighteenth-century rococo, with many recollections of Correggio; and a Head Piece by Bartolozzi, entitled "Invocation," recalls Guido's "Aurora." Nor is the antique absent, for Celadon has a Roman face and Musidora is a classical statue. At the same time the newer woodland sentimentalism appears in "Parental Affection": cottagers serve one another in a tonally extravagant piece that sets the figures against a dark forest. In similar engravings the cottage and the spinning wheel, peasant superstitions, wild nature, and happy countrymen illustrate the successful formula of the sentimental picturesque.

To all the tendencies that appear in this volume Blake the painter-poet made responses that help us define his identity.

THE PICTURESQUE

Blake was not predisposed to landscape, but he did have before his eyes the brilliant careers of three contemporary engravers, whom he knew personally and whom he came to loathe as toadies of fashionable taste. John Hall, who died in 1797, engraved historical paintings after Benjamin West and also reproduced the romantic scenes of Hamilton, De Loutherbourg, and Gibbon in brilliant works of chiaroscuro where tone, not line, defines form. Sir Robert Strange, who died in 1792, did portraits, allegories, and histories after Guido Reni, but also richly romantic scenes after Wouwerman and Salvator Rosa. But perhaps it was William Woollett (1735–85) who brought preromantic engraving to a tonal brilliance hitherto unmatched, making, in fact, the burin and the acid rivals of the brush and pigment. Beginning, like Blake himself and his master Basire, with topographical and architectural views, he soon found that the dark forest, clouds, shadows, shimmering, almost immaterial, trees, water in various lights, and atmospheric ruins challenged his skill more than anything else. His etchings and engravings (Plate XXXIX) of the landscapes of Jean Pillement, Claude, Richard Wilson, Richard Wright, De Loutherbourg, George Smith, and others brought picturesque engraving to a standard not attained until Turner and his associates put landscapes onto copper by etching and mezzotint in his *Liber Studiorum* (begun in 1807), truly one of the climaxes of romantic naturalism in art. Woollett, unlike Strange, engraved relatively few histories, even fewer allegories, and in the collection of his works at the British Museum there are no Guidos, Raphaels, Michelangelos. Woollett instead devoted his great talents to the picturesque, adapting heroic landscape to local scenes and the English past. Blake's dislike[2] of the man may have been in part personal, but it cannot have been unrelated to the fact that Woollett was a tonal, not a linear, artist, who subordinated man to landscape, symbolic meaning to purely natural phenomena.

Blake rejected the romantic picturesque, but he was exposed to it early and constantly. William Pars, the brother of Henry Pars, whose drawing school in the Strand Blake attended, painted English landscape and architecture and also classical, Turkish, and Swiss scenes, some of which were engraved by Woollett himself. James Basire, Blake's master, engraved, and taught his apprentice to engrave, classical and medieval architecture and to endow these scenes with at least a suspicion of the coming picturesque. But his competent though somewhat crabbed style set no such an example as that of Woollett and Strange. To Basire's more modest but more humanistic and traditional view Blake remained a lifelong devotee, even though now and then he might engrave a romantic landscape after a fashionable artist like George Morland.[3]

Blake's objections to the picturesque were philosophical as well as aesthetic. Naturalistic art and poetry were necessarily involved in natural objects, which Blake said weakened or obliterated his imagination.[4] In fact, the only occasion on which he seems to have agreed with Reynolds arose when the president, in a letter to Gilpin, declared the picturesque to be a matter of taste and not genius, a quality in second-rate artists like Pope and Prior, far below the grandeur of a Milton or a Michelangelo. "So Says Sir Joshua," exclaimed Blake, "and So say I."[5]

[2] Public Address (*c.* 1810), *CW*, pp. 593, 594, 600, 603.
[3] Archibald G. B. Russell, *The Engravings of William Blake* (London, 1912), p. 151.
[4] Blake to Crabb Robinson in Arthur Symons, *William Blake* (London, 1907), p. 300.
[5] Letter to Butts, November 22, 1802, *CW*, p. 814

Henry Fuseli distinguished three kinds of landscape—"the transcript of a spot, or a picturesque combination of homogeneous objects, or the scene of a phenomenon."[6] The first kind Blake produced as an apprentice; the third kind appeared in the Felpham passages of *Milton*, where cottage and seaside were hallowed by divine visitations. But for the "picturesque combination of homogeneous objects" Blake had nothing but contempt. Gilpin considered words and paintings "gross, insipid substitutes of the living scene."[7] Blake considered the merely natural scene a gross and insipid substitute for mental reality and would have none of it until the living word and line had elevated it to meaning.

ALLEGORIES AND HISTORIES

Blake, along with Cromek, Bartolozzi, and others, engraved for popular literary works the designs of Richard Westall, Angelica Kauffmann, Lady Diana Beauclerk, Cosway, Maria Flaxman, Romney, and Metz.[8] These sometimes sank to portraying society allegories with simpering cupids—the very nadir of the rococo—but sometimes rose to fairly sophisticated visual personifications appropriate to the preromantic Miltonists, if not to Milton himself.

Blake was most obviously connected with the school of fashionable allegory by his many engravings after Thomas Stothard, an early political as well as artistic friend. Some of their joint labors resulted in fashionable *conversazioni* arising from literary narrative, as in the illustrations of *Don Quixote*; other work reflects the persisting influence of Hogarth. At their worst Stothard's illustrations place preposterous medieval cavaliers and white-clad society ladies in the wooded parks of English country estates or fill the sky with allegorical heads derived academically from Raphael, Guido Reni, Correggio, or the antique. But Stothard's imagination did now and then lead him beyond the defects of his school to authentic echoes of the greater tradition from which he and his fellows sprang, and some of Blake's engravings after Stothard have unmistakably Blakean touches in the design—because Blake added them himself or

[6] Aphorism No. 236 in John Knowles, *The Life and Writings of Henry Fuseli* (London, 1831), III, 147.

[7] William Gilpin, *Observations . . . on Several Parts of England, Particularly . . . Cumberland and Westmoreland* (London, 1786), II, 11.

[8] See Russell, *op. cit.* (n. 3), *passim.*

because he selected those designs that came closest to his own ideals or because collaboration was intimate from the beginning of the process.

Bartolozzi, a representative engraver of the allegorical school, provides another instructive contrast. Where Blake was linear, Bartolozzi was tonal. Blake's personifications arose from the depths of a subconscious fed by the Book of Revelation; Bartolozzi's came from rococo canvases or the fashionable salons and remained at the top of his mind. Blake was inspired by Dürer, Raphael, Michelangelo, and Giulio. Bartolozzi attached himself to the Raphael of the Madonnas, Correggio, Guercino, the Carracci, Maratti, Poussin, Carlo Dolci, Domenichino, Giordano, and Le Brun.

It is easy today to dismiss the school of fashionable allegory and history by contrasting its sentimental weaknesses with Blake's robustness. But even though it did not affect his artistic health, this movement did provide a milieu that left its traces on even his best work and that was by no means as disreputable as is sometimes thought. The *Josephus* of about 1785, which appeared three years or so before Blake began illuminating his own work and which contained three of his engravings, is a work of considerable dignity and power—and, what is more to the point, of some relevance to the later Blake. The frontispiece (Metz-Grignion) is a baroque allegory that unites a Raphaelesque face and personified abstractions from Ripa in a manner that, though it lacks great animation, is basically Blakean in pattern. The creation scenes, with their mystical signs, are more allegorical and emblematic than Blake ever was, and the Stothard-Blake illustrating Joshua 8:20 is much more purely a history piece than Blake alone ever undertook. But in the representation of the fugitive Shechemites (Metz engraved by Blake) the landscape—a hillside burrowed with caves, a murky sky streaked with bats and owls—is strikingly Blakean (Plate XXXVIIIA). Even when Blake's burin is not involved, one has the feeling of being in the foothills that lead to his mountains: Samuel in the Salvator-Noble "Witch of Endor" is a bearded patriarch, Urizenic in manner (Plate XXXVIIIB); the lions that lie around Daniel in another piece bear the subdued fierceness of the lions and tigers of Innocence and Experience.[9]

9 *The Whole Genuine and Complete Works of Flavius Josephus*, ed. George Henry Maynard and Edward Kimpton (London, [1785–86]), pp. 7, 64–65, 76, 96, 161.

Blake outgrew fashionable allegory and even came to hate it. But it had early engaged his hand and mind, and he always remained related to it if for no other reason than that he drank pure from the high Renaissance what his colleagues and contemporaries drank adulterated as Bolognese eclecticism, French aestheticism, and English academicism. If Blake was more violent in his reaction to popular history-painting than to the picturesque—to Reynolds, say, than to Gainsborough—it was surely because "pessimus corruptio optimi"—because prostituting Raphael or Michelangelo was blasphemous while warming over Claude Lorrain was only contemptible.

THE SCHOOL OF BLAKE

None of Blake's relations is so obvious as the one that linked him to what has been called the school of the "Neoclassic Horrific" [10] but what may more properly be called the "School of Blake," the genitive being both subjective and objective in proportions hard to determine. Barry, Mortimer, and Fuseli constituted his most intimate and immediate context. These men were contemporaries and friends, influenced by the same works, often sharing the same political and artistic ideals, borrowing from one another, and making no secret of their mutual approbation.

James Barry (d. 1806) and Blake had much in common as men. Both were republican in political faith and supported the freedom of Americans, French, Africans, women, and slaves. Artistically, the two also made common cause. They both scorned Benjamin West, who they thought had debased history-painting to flatter a living monarch. They both shared antiquarian interests, and Barry's representations of openmouthed horror, like Blake's, may derive from the Roman tragic mask. Both loved the nude and believed that mythic heroic action could best be conveyed by bare bodies in powerful motion. Both loved Milton and hated contemporary religious and artistic officialdom.

These general affiliations are supported by particular parallels so close that one suspects direct influence. Lear's hair in Barry's engraving for Boydell is blown to one side, as Urizen-God's is in

---

[10] Mimeographed catalogue of the Blake Bicentenary Exhibition (1957), at the British Museum, "William Blake and His Circle," p. 20.

the frontispiece to *Europe*. Barry's powerful drawing of Sin, Death, and Satan anticipates Blake's. Barry's "Job," in which the patriarch is reproved by his friends, one of whom points an accusing finger, has helped form Blake's superior scene (Plate XLB). Barry's youthful Lucifer calling to his legions as he stands proudly on the edge of a rock is in the spirit of the Blake's revolutionary Satanism. Barry's Orpheus, like Blake's Los, is a tamer of the "Tyger's fierceness and the Lion's Rage" and brings to the state of nature the civilizing effects of art. Barry's serene religious scenes, in pen and India ink over red chalk, present lovely human figures—Joseph, Mary, Jesus, John, standing in a lightly drawn landscape, which their strongly outlined bodies clearly dominate. Barry's minstrel, derived from Beattie, anticipates Blake's visual rendering of the youthful poet, both in his posture and in his Dürer-like natural setting where trees stand high and roots emerge from rocks that tower above the human figures' heads. Barry's head of Neptune (Plate XLA)—with sightless, statuesque eyes, with long, ropy beard, flowing from the nostrils and dividing the lip, with moustaches that end in dolphins' heads, with the thick lips parted in the manner of a mask—anticipates Blake's equally frightening presentations of aged evil and make one wonder whether Barry too saw an oppressive society behind ancient statuary. Personal indignation and social satire make Barry's "Judas returning the Bribe" a Blakean sermon. (The high priest is worldly, complacent; Judas is frightened and deeply agitated—an example, Barry says in a note at the bottom of the picture, of "corrupt Influence operating upon Weak Virtue.") These resemblances may explain why Blake once compared Barry to Raphael.[11]

John Hamilton Mortimer's career, which ended in 1779, when Blake's apprenticeship terminated, and which Blake defended even though it was "Dissipated and Wild," may have been a Satanist in life as well as in art. The picturesque and eccentric painter of heroic histories, who lived for a while above the auction rooms that Blake frequented as a boy, was the kind of tough-minded satirist of society and uninhibited creator of evil monsters that Blake must have admired and studied. Both men were literary painters, whose inspirations came from poetry, epic and mythic, and from the Bible.

[11] Quoted by David Erdman, *Blake Prophet against Empire* (Princeton, 1954), p. 38.

Both had keen, angry, unsentimental, and vigorously protestant social consciences. Both loved the grotesque and were fascinated by the strain of bodies in terrible struggle against evil. Both, though they loved to use natural settings emblematically, were unpicturesque line-artists who made the human figure, real or allegorical, dominate the environment. Mortimer, like Barry—occasionally in untypical peaceful scenes, more often in violent mythological or biblical actions—composed histories that prefigured Blake's prophetic visualizations. But, unlike Barry, Mortimer runs often to single heads and individual figures. Shakespeare's Edgar—who is accompanied by an appropriate motto, who stares a mad stare, whose mouth is parted to show his teeth, whose hands bear a sheaf of wheat, whose head is covered with grain and leaves—is an outcast of Nature. Cassandra, from Shakespeare's *Troilus*, her eyes wild, her lips parted in horror, displays only her head. Shylock, his lips open, his forehead creased in frowns, displays glaring but cunning eyes. Ophelia's madness is conveyed by lips, eyes, and cheeks. Richard II, his eyes staring, his beard curly, wears a crown spiked in Blakean fashion, within which sits a skeleton with a crown of leaves, holding a pin which he is ready to plunge into any opening he can find. Some figures—Belisarius, Don Quixote—remain men, but others are monsters: men's heads with reptile tails and webbed feet, lewd, hateful, vengeful creatures, the products of the artist's rage. These powerfully rendered figures from literature, perhaps the products of the popular aesthetic notion that painting is at its best when it expresses ideas through muscle and feature, constitute Mortimer's most striking achievement.

Mortimer anticipates Blake. But the fact that he also recalls the Giulio Romano of the Palazzo del T and the Goltzius of the chiaroscuro woodcuts leads one to wonder if perhaps the English artist was not in fact the transmitter of the grotesque horrors and the violent dramatic actions of the earlier artists to his younger contemporary. For one of Mortimer's male figures wears a mailed coat that suggests the fish scales of Giulio Romano's—and Blake's —soldiers. Mortimer's "Nebuchadnezzar" (Plate XLIA) has been said to recall Dürer's and Cranach's "St. Jerome" and to anticipate Blake's animalized monarch (Plate LIB); but it is closer in style and spirit—as is his violent action, "Ajax bestriding the Dead Body of Patroclus"—to the wild and powerful nude men that Hendrick Goltzius places in his caves and on his rocks.[12]

In 1764 a brilliant young Swiss eccentric, an ex-pastor from Zurich, a pupil of Bodmer and Breitinger, a preromantic who wished to use Milton, Shakespeare, Thomson, and Young to emancipate German literature from French classicism, first came to London as Heinrich Füssli. He died in England in 1825 as Henry Fuseli, a permanent part of English culture, an indispensable ingredient in English romanticism. Perhaps his most enduring creation was whatever in William Blake he quickened into artistic life. Blake, who admired him, followed him, quarreled with him, and finally surpassed him, was of course no carbon copy of the older man; and on many large matters their differences were profound. Gothic art, which for Blake became a symbol of the imaginative life, was to Fuseli an abomination; and Greek art, which for Blake became a symbol of war and repression, was for Fuseli one of the few truly valid expressions of the human spirit. Fuseli valued Reynolds—his notes on Dufresnoy the Swiss artist called "treasures of practical observation"[13]—but Blake made the president of the Royal Society a symbol of all that was wrong with the official art and the ruling classes of England. Fuseli considered those Blakean villains, Correggio and Titian, important members of the pantheon; found it possible to praise Rubens, whom Blake loathed; and censured, in terms of official doctrine, the vagaries of one of Blake's heroes, Albrecht Dürer. It is not impossible that the friendship which during the decade of the nineties had been so intimate and fructifying later cooled, as Fuseli came to dislike what contained the very ichor of Blake's inner being, the Prophetic Books.

But for all that, Fuseli is more Blakean than anyone except Blake himself, partly because he owed much to Blake (he once said the younger man was very good to steal from) but mostly because Blake

[12] On Mortimer, see *ibid.*, pp. 37–38. Particular works mentioned in the text were examined in the British Museum, Department of Prints and Drawings.

[13] *Lectures on Painting by the Royal Academicians. Barry, Opie, and Fuseli*, ed. Ralph N. Wornum (London, 1889), p. 344. On Fuseli, see also Knowles (*op. cit.* [n. 6]); Eudo C. Mason, *The Mind of Henry Fuseli* (London, 1951); Frederick Antal, *Fuseli Studies* (London, 1956); Ruthven Todd, *Tracks in the Snow* (New York, 1947); the collections in the British Museum; and his illustrations to Pope's *Rape of the Lock* (1798), Cowper's poems (1806), Pope's *Homer* (1805), Cowper's *Iliad* and *Odyssey* (1810).

owed so much to him (Plate XLII). Blake and Fuseli shared a devotion to Shakespeare, Milton, and preromantic poetry that never flowered into an appreciation of romanticism itself; and they were united by common pictorial enthusiasms. Raphael stood high, but not, as in neoclassical judgment, at the very top. That eminence was reserved for Michelangelo, and it is not unlikely that Blake was led deep into his understanding of the Italian genius by his older friend, himself the most Michelangelesque of English painters, who had seen the Sistine masterpieces with his own eyes as he lay on his back in the Vatican chapel. Both Blake and Fuseli blazed in anger at those pallid academicians who dared profess admiration for the titan they could not possibly have understood. Blake and Fuseli may also have shared a taste for the Mannerist art that separated the high Renaissance and the Baroque. The same Goltzius, whose chiaroscuro woodcuts bear such striking resemblance to the prophetic Blake, Fuseli admired for his very deviations from accepted norms—"the eccentricities and extremes of the great style." [14]

These shared admirations rested on the common conviction that historical and allegorical art of heroic ambition was as superior to landscape and portrait as imagination was to nature. Blake's denigration of natural objects as damps on his imagination is matched by Fuseli's outburst: "Damn nature—she always puts me out."

Fuseli's drawings and paintings show the profoundest relationships to Blake's art. Both men use the clear, bounding outline. In both, human figures dominate landscape. Both create highly original, even eccentric and perverse, personifications of natural and mental phenomena. Both place human forms in unnatural but powerfully expressive postures, on the earth and in the air. And both are concerned, not so much with the supernatural as with the "inter-natural," the "infra-natural." That is, both men explore, with an uncanny sense of depth, rightness, and relation of parts, the interior psyche in such a way as to recall the mannerists and now and then to anticipate even the surrealists. Dreams unite disparate natural details to produce monstrosities. Fetal postures recall the womb. Bodies unite in embraces that in Fuseli are erotic and in Blake erotic-religious. Besides exploring the soul in nightmare, in vision, and in dreamy recollections of the archetype, both men satirize society.

[14] Antal, *op. cit.* (n. 13), p. 102.

Blake's entire vision is socially and politically oriented. Fuseli's coarse, erotic, surrealistically distorted women assume the postures of fine society—ghoulish figures before the mirror or in the drawing room, disposed in ways that mock fashionable rococo and neoclassical art. Bald men, at once goatish and conventional, symbolize war and social evil. In the engravings that were made after Fuseli for the literary works of Homer, Cowper, Milton, and Shakespeare, Fuseli practices a visual rendition of words that is highly Blakean. Both men were attracted by the melodramatic and spectacular scene and by heroic gesture and unnatural, theatrical posture. They most unmistakably depart from the inhibited and tiresome literary engravings of their day in their attempts to visualize the most intractable verbal materials. Neither was deterred from rendering an author's moral abstractions and poetical fancies—his abstract generalizations, metaphysical metaphors, unnatural personifications, embedded meanings.

Cowper described moral qualities in the manner of the mid-eighteenth-century poet by a series of personifications, some more, some less pictorial.

> Both baby-featured, and of infant size,
> Viewed from a distance, and with heedless eyes,
> Folly and innocence are so alike,
> The difference, though essential, fails to strike.
> Yet folly ever has a vacant stare,
> A simpering countenance, and a trifling air;
> But innocence, sedate, serene, erect,
> Delights us, by engaging our respect.[15]

Ignoring the attributes, "baby-featured" and "of infant size," and leaving out innocence altogether as an unsurmountable irrelevance to a unified visual scene, Fuseli, following Cowper's series of three predicate phrases, represents folly by three persons, all the same height, each dressed in white (Plate XLIB). The woman to the extreme right "has a vacant stare"; the middle figure has "a simpering countenance" as she holds a finger to her lip and looks coquettish; and the third woman, before the mirror, attended by a maid, has "a trifling air." Fuseli enriches Cowper's straightforward morality with irony by recollecting two famous pictorial themes, Venus at the Mirror and the Three Graces.

[15] From "Progress of Error" in *Poems by William Cowper* (London, 1806), I, 51.

When the text is more brilliant and imaginative than Cowper's, Fuseli follows his author closely and emulates Pope's witty and allusive richness, as Umbriel flies away from the goddess Spleen, carrying the bag of sighs in one hand and the vial of fears in the other. Fuseli's Umbriel spreads his black wings, as Spleen, lying in bed, averts her head but extends her hand. Though she is dressed in white, filmy gauze, the place is as gloomy as Pope describes it. Megrim holds his head in his hands and rests his elbows on the bed. Pain, a shadowy figure, with an emaciated face, stands by, just barely emerging from the gloom. Ill Nature sits at the foot reading a Prayer Book, wearing a ring and a black and white gown. Affectation hangs her head, wears a simpering look, sinks to her knees, caresses a lap dog with one hand and holds a fan in the other, the last details coming from elsewhere in the poem. The living teapot stands on the floor. The pipkin looks like a man with a stovepipe hat, as he walks with legs apart. The maid turned bottle is a tiny woman, gauzily gowned, kneeling on one knee and playing a lute. There are no pictorial lakes of liquid gold, crystal domes, or angels in machines; but the glaring fiend and rolling snake appear in the rearing serpent that accompanies Umbriel's upward flight, whose mouth is open and whose one visible eye glares white.

Such illustrations—so daring, so unconventional, and sometimes so mistaken—provided the closest analogues to Blake's treatment of the written word, his own and others'.

From Barry and Mortimer to Blake are but two short steps, from Fuseli but one. Their art illumines many but not all sides of Blake's genius. He must be given a wider context than that which his contemporaries can provide. Fuseli and his school seldom suggest the *Songs of Innocence and Experience* or *The Book of Thel*, but appropriate medieval illuminations do. Nor are the designs of the contemporaries, however bold in rendering poetical personifications, ever emblematic in the compact, gnomic, and childishly didactic manner of Blake and his seventeenth-century predecessors. And although Blake's contemporaries reinforced the impressions of the high Renaissance masters and even reinterpreted them for him, his contact with Raphael, Michelangelo, and Giulio Romano—as engraved by Marcantonio and the chiaroscuro colorists—was early, enduring, firsthand, and independent.

The tradition we have traced from the middle of the fifteenth century to the late eighteenth century is integral because Blake's vision made it so. He used his predecessors with the firm purpose of a thinker and artist—of a *composite* artist. For Blake drew on no graphic artist who was not intellectually or verbally oriented. Illuminations and emblems united word and design. Often Dürer's engraved masterpieces were accompanied by the biblical or historical texts they illustrated, and Blake's contemporaries were illustrators more than they were anything else. Even Raphael, Giulio Romano, and Michelangelo, as Blake saw them, were primarily the creators of biblical and mythological histories, not of madonnas, pietàs, portraits, or luminous landscapes.

PART II

Blake's Illuminations

CHAPTER VI

Innocence and Experience

In 1788—a date he remembered many years later as the beginning of his career in illumination—Blake published three works of stereotyped engraving: two series entitled "There Is No Natural Religion" and one entitled "All Religions Are One." Each of the twenty-five or so unbound sheets that comprise the series—these are the tiniest engravings (measuring 2 × 2.5 inches) Blake ever made—contains a short proverb, embellished with a border and a top or bottom design. The entire series is unified in subject matter, and those details that are clear enough to be seen appear to complement one another. Blake has produced a series of artistically successful emblems—economical in expression, intellectually sophisticated, morally serious.

The proverbs (or "Principles," as they are called in the second of these works) attack the rationalistic empiricism of the eighteenth century—by implication, Locke, Newton, Hume—and recommend the religion of the imagination, for already in Blake's thought psychology leads to art and art to religion. The first series of the first work reduces the sensationist psychology to absurdity: the man governed only by the senses is confined to a dull repetition in life and art of only material reality. The second series of the first work expresses the hunger of man for the infinite and establishes a contrast between the man who sees God in all things and the man who sees only himself—his own senses and his own reason. "All Religions Are One" equates the imagination with the perception of the infinite; man's ability to create establishes his uniqueness as man and lies behind all true religion. These aphorisms express one of the fundamental antitheses of Blake's thought—between the "Poetic or Prophetic character" and the "Philosophical & Experimental"; between the natural man and the spiritual man, to use St.

Paul's language, between Christ-Los and Urizen-Satan, to use Blake's.

Blake's first illuminations come early in his career, but he had even earlier anticipated the contrasts between the way of neoclassical reason and the way of the liberating imagination. The Poetic-Prophetic character, always associated with the lover, had been adumbrated in the *Poetical Sketches:* in the prince of love, "who in the sunny beams did glide"; in the poetic type, doubtless influenced by Gray, who "pores upon the stream / Where sighing lovers dream," and who walks with "silent Melancholy"; in the Collins-like personifications of spring, summer, and the sun; and in the poet-traveler who comes back to his own country to die and receive the forgiveness of the mother who bore him. By the time Blake came to annotate Lavater and Swedenborg, he had fully developed the idea of an antithesis between "abstraction" and "Christian philosophy," between the natural man (who is condemned by "worldly wisdom" and the "bodily Senses" to "meer Nature or Hell") and the Poetic Genius (which discerns God in the lowest effects as well as in the highest causes and which sees that "every thing on earth is the word of God & in its essence is God").[1]

Blake was convinced early that "it is impossible to think without images of somewhat on earth." You cannot love a white cloud, but you can love a holy man within the cloud.[2] Abstract thought creates monsters, the affections create images and persons. Blake had accepted the central doctrine of the preromantic school, and in these, the earliest engravings of his own work, his habit of personifying found expression in the visual designs that accompany the paradoxical proverbs. These forms are not vague, eccentric, or unrelated strokes of the pencil; they firmly support the particular subject of each plate and the general subject of the series. Design expresses the central antithesis no less forcibly than the words. On the side of Sense-Reason, which reduces man to stifling materialism, are the woman whose eyes are blindfolded by a cloth; the bearded figure lying on the ground writing in a book (a clear anticipation of one of Urizen's most characteristic postures and acts); the dark,

[1] *CW*, pp. 1, 2, 3, 6, 8, 36, 65, 87, 93.
[2] *CW*, pp. 88, 90.

barren trees or stumps with creepers that, serpentlike, embrace them; the barren branches that form round arches over the pages; the bent old man who leans on a stick and looks at the dog on the ground; the old man with arms akimbo (another of Urizen's favorite positions); the curlicues in the borders that suggest serpents; and the tablets of the law (Plate VD). The Poetic Imagination is symbolized by the child from whose hands a bird escapes to freedom; the winged cupid who points upward; the child who with open arms runs toward a swan; the sheep who graze at the bottom of the design; every suggestion of Gothic form; and the Poetic Youth, who pipes a pipe under a tree, who supports himself by resting his arm in the crotch of the tree, who sits nude in an arbor, who rises from the ground (Plate VB), and who as a traveler wears a broad-brimmed hat and carries a walking stick as he strides boldly through the landscape (Plate VC).

The two contrary states are not only separately symbolized. They have been worked into a tightly knit coherence: sometimes the design duplicates what the words say—the word "travelling" is paralleled by a traveler—(Plate VC); more often, the designs complement the words in such a way as to insure that on almost every plate, if one takes into account border and design as well as word, Blake's entire paradox is represented. The sixth principle of "All Religions Are One" says that "The Jewish & Christian Testaments are An original derivation from the Poetic Genius; this is necessary from the confined nature of bodily sensation" (Plate VD). Above these words Blake has represented the Jewish Testament in tiny tablets, among Blake's firmest symbols of perverted religion—a perversion only hinted at by the last phrase of the text. Below the words a mantled figure in white strides through the landscape, one of Blake's permanent symbols for the Poetic Genius. Thus the contrast implicit in the aphorism—between the "confined nature of bodily sensation" and the "Poetic Genius"—is expressed in the top and bottom designs. In the seventh principle of the second series of "There Is No Natural Religion" ("The desire of Man being Infinite, the possession is Infinite & himself Infinite") the spray of leaves at the top and the figure rising with the sprays with arms outstretched symbolize the desire for the infinite (Plate VB). In the plate immediately following, the "Application" ("He who sees the Infinite in all things sees God. He who sees the

Ratio[3] only, sees himself only"), the design illustrates the second clause: a figure at bottom kneels on the ground, to which he applies a geometer's compass—an anticipation of Blake's famous mathematical deity in the frontispiece to *Europe*.

INNOCENCE

Only one year separated Blake's beginning in composite art from his greatest masterpiece in that medium, the *Songs of Innocence*. This imperishable work—perhaps even more beautiful in its early simple coloring, where tender shades harmonize with the mood, than in the more lavish coloring of later issues—rests on the foundation of a dignified and coherent concept. Innocence recalls Eden and anticipates the New Jerusalem. Natural life flowers in uninhibited sexuality; and all its forms, vegetable, animal, and human, are holy to the imagination of the poet, who appears as piper and shepherd and in whose vision, at its burning core, stands Christ as child, lamb, or lion.

Of these three integrally related elements of Innocence—humble life, natural sexuality, the Poet-Christ—*humble life* is the particular province of the border, which is here lusher, richer, and more beautiful in itself than on any other of Blake's pages.

The woods of Arcady were far from dead. They had in childhood surrounded Blake and all others of his generation and all previous generations. And in the arts they constituted a rich heritage. Some of the suggestions that came to Blake were poetic: Milton's "gadding vine" and "twisted eglantine," for example, and the "gray-fly (who) winds her sultry horn." Others were pictorial. Among Blake's contemporaries, including Constable and Turner, the tree border, with entwining branches or trunks, was a visual cliché. Blake's organic life is more emblematic than any other artist's—more certainly than in landscape where it was often aesthetically rich but philosophically imprecise, more even than in the emblem where it was, though symbolical, sparse and austere. In Blake's borders, with trees, vines, creepers, leaves, birds, and

---

[3] By *ratio* Blake means the mental process that reasons only about sensations, the faculty that discovered the truth in neoclassical empirical rationalism. *Ratio* was thus a pejorative term. But there is a higher reason: "Reason, or A Ratio of All we have Known, is not the Same as it shall be when we know More"—a sentence that attacks Reynolds's repetition of the eighteenth-century cliché that "reason is something invariable and fixed in the nature of things" *CW*, p. 475.

insects, life was abundant—and allusive. Even the letters of the title page vegetate into organic forms, and organic forms elsewhere resemble flames. For all that lives is holy, and tongues of living fire had immemorially been associated with Pentecost and with divine and poetic inspiration.

The second ingredient of Blake's Innocence, *uninhibited sexuality*, appears alike in word, border, and design. Lamb and ewe call to each other in the exquisite verse. Leaf and stem, as in "The Blossom" and "Infant Joy," suggests the phallus erect and in repose; the flower suggests the womb. The boy on the second page of "The Ecchoing Green" who hands grapes from a vine to a girl on the ground is an emblem of sexual awareness (Plate XXXV). Lyca's solitary experiences in the forest were sexual, as the embrace of man and woman on the first page of "The Little Girl Lost" seems to suggest.

The *Poet-Christ* of Innocence manifests himself in different ways but nowhere more fundamentally than in the equation of the Poetic and Prophetic characters, of divine love and human imagination. The Poet of the frontispiece, who lowers his pipe at the vision, is entirely human; the child on a cloud just above his head is both natural and divine, as are the Lamb of the fields and the Infant born in a flower. All those who rescue the lost and the wayfaring are manifestations of the divine shepherd who seeks and finds the straying sheep: the father, who saves the little boy led astray by Blake's version of Wordsworth's "unfathered vapour that enwraps,/ At once, some lonely traveller";[4] the lonely watchman of the night, who brings the wandering emmet back to her children; and the lordly lion, who protects the lost Lyca and who reconciles the grieving parents to separation from their daughter.

Blake's Innocence has a quality that makes it poignant—its capacity for being blighted by society. There passes now and then over it the shadow of Experience, a cloud that suggests the coming dark but that does not destroy the day. Blake had suggested some two years before that a man might be offended with "the innocence of a child . . . , because it reproaches him with the errors of acquired folly." [5] These songs do in fact rebuke the adult and the institutional enemies of Innocence who will one day destroy it.

[4] *Prelude* vi. 595–96.
[5] "Annotations to Lavater," *CW*, p. 87.

79

That destruction Blake unmistakably adumbrates even in the borders. When his close friend Cumberland noted that the vine grasps "the distorted trunk with *snaky* twine,"[6] he provided the proper perspective on one of the most insistent visual motifs in the *Songs of Innocence*. For in border and design, tree twists around tree, creeper and vine embrace trunk, vine and stem rise in serpentine loops and often form round, Urizenic arches over the page. The entire tradition that Blake absorbed—from illuminated missal to Fuseli, from the Bible through Milton to his master James Basire— suggests that the twisting serpentine forms of his Edenic garden prefigure a Fall.

So solidly conceived is Blake's idea of Innocence and so richly is it supported in border, word, and design that it alone succeeds in making the *Songs of Innocence* an integrated and serious work of art. But the book succeeds also because of the incomparable excellence of many of its individual pages—successes that Blake was to repeat but never to surpass.

The pages of *Innocence* are of three kinds, not equally complex or rich but each capable of appropriate artistic distinction. The kinds may be called *illustration*, *decoration*, and *illumination*—terms here applied to Blake's single pages and only distantly related to their use elsewhere in the art of bookmaking.

Illustration refers to the most conventional form Blake employed, in which the design—sometimes literal, sometimes based on the metaphor of the poem, and sometimes capable of introducing persons and scenes not clearly in the poem—appears at the top, bottom, or middle of the page. The mother, the child, the chair, and the cradle of the tailpiece reproduce the scene of "A Cradle Song." In the worthy but somewhat slack and sentimental "Little Black Boy," the boy and his mother appear in the top design at the water's edge looking at what must be an emblematic sunrise, and the white boy and the black boy appear with Christ in the tailpiece. In "The Chimney Sweeper," the boys' vision of air and angels—not the work-a-day world of soot, bags, brushes, and chimneys that oppresses them—is represented at the foot of the page.

Sometimes simple illustration is masterfully integrated with the total form of the page. The first of two exquisite plates devoted to

[6] George Cumberland, *A Poem on the Landscapes of Great Britain* (London, 1793), p. 9.

"Spring" begins with a representation at the top of a child "welcoming the year" by stretching his hands out to the sheep while he is still held by his mother, who sings the first two stanzas. The second page, in a balancing tailpiece that is tied to the headpiece by simple looping borders, shows the child alone without his mother fondling the lambs—an appropriate accompaniment to the last stanza in which the child speaks: "Little Lamb, / Here I am."

This kind of illustration also contributes to Blake's total concept of Innocence by reminding us of the world of children and naïve experience, where ideas are simplified by pictures and already simple word scenes are made even simpler by color and line.

Decoration uses only text and border. Border designs, usually in the same color as the engraved text, reinforce the abstract, metaphoric meaning. (Some borders have tiny angels or *putti* in the decorative motifs, but these do not destroy the essential abstractness of the design.) The exquisite borders of the "Introduction" stylize exuberant organic life, one of the basic ingredients of Innocence. "On Another's Sorrow" adds to rich natural life serpentine adumbrations of Experience and supports textual references to the crucifixion of Christ. The first page of "Night," which possesses a visual tact Blake did not always display, chooses from a rich variety of verbal images—wolves, tigers, King Lion, a flood of moonlight, and a vision of the future—only tiny border angels descending in darkness. In "A Dream" Blake's border grows thicker around the title—on whose "A" and "D" two tiny forms sleep—and around the first lines, "Once a dream did weave a shade / O'er my Angel-guarded bed." In "A Cradle Song" the border vegetation also forms a shade that delicately repeats the shade formed by infant dreams in the opening lines.

Blake most triumphantly realizes his form in *illumination*, the kind of page that unites border and design in a single visual motif. That motif bounds the page, separates stanzas, represents figures and scenes from the texts, and both literally and metaphorically winds itself around the words. "Infant Joy" (Plate XLIII), "The Divine Image," and "The Blossom" are in this sense illuminations, authentic and unsurpassed masterpieces of fully integrated composite art.[7]

7 I have been anticipated by Anthony Blunt (*The Art of William Blake* [New York, 1959], p. 48).

"The Divine Image" (Plate XLIV) separates deity into its four component virtues—those four daughters of the voice of God: Mercy, Pity, Peace, and Love. It asserts that the God who embodies these virtues becomes man and that the man who embodies them becomes God. Such interpenetration of the divine and the human brings with it the ethical imperative that "all must love the human form / In heathen, turk, or jew." The organizing formal element in the design is a green flame-plant that rises from lower right to upper left, forming borders as it rises. Embraced by a delicate flowering convolvulus that may presage the coming Fall, the plant is an organic version of Jacob's ladder that unites heaven and earth. From heaven descends a robed lady, clearly a goddess, attended by a flying joy—a tiny personified aurora that precedes the dawn. As God becomes man—or woman, really—in the upper left, man becomes God in lower right, for Christ raises two figures from the ground—two human beings who will leave the cave of distress to climb the plant upward. Two tiny figures near the top represent the men of every clime who pray in their distress. In the poem mankind is called simply man and the divinity simply God. But in the elaborating design mankind is presented as a man and a woman, while God is presented at the bottom as Christ and at the top in female form. The presence of both sexes reminds us that one of the four divine attributes is Love, that Blake's Innocence is a world of natural sexuality, and that this particular poem recommends "virtues of delight."

Of equal profundity and even greater unity is "The Blossom" (Plate XLV). The words seem to describe a merry sparrow, a happy blossom, and a grieving robin, but the designs imply sexual love. The flame-flower could be phallic; tiny cupids have taken the place of the textual sparrow, who appears nowhere in the design; a child with his mother has replaced the similarly absent robin; and one of the cupids rides, not a serpent as in *Thel*, but one of the leaves, or tongues, of the flame-plant. These love themes in the picture unlock the meaning of the words: the merry sparrow who seeks his narrow cradle with the swiftness of an arrow is an exquisite rendition of sexual experience, and the sobbing robin is an equally exquisite rendition of mother-love and child-sorrow. The blossom is, in the first stanza, wife, in the second, mother. An appropriate epigraph comes from *The Marriage of Heaven and Hell*, "Joys impregnate. Sorrows bring forth." [8]

EXPERIENCE

Experience is blighted Innocence. It is not a period of horrible but healthy probation, a purgatory we must inevitably traverse en route to the heavenly kingdom. It is a congregation of social, political, psychological, and unnatural horrors, a pestilential state whose vapors sicken the soul. The one ray of light that penetrates its darkness is that of the coming judgment that will destroy it.

Blake's most obvious sign of man's perverted state appears in the borders—in the vegetation with which he surrounds text and design. In *Innocence* it was fresh, attractive, abundant; in *Experience* it recalls the earlier ripeness but is in fact dead or dying. The tree of *Innocence* is large and healthy, its branches entwined in a natural embrace; but it anticipates the Fall in the serpentine creeper that often winds about its trunk. The tree of *Experience* is dry and dying, its withering branches form round arches over the page as its spiky twigs invade the text; but its shape and the few sprays that still shoot recall its primal vigor (see Plates XLVI, LIVA, LXVIB). Experience is related to Innocence as a fossil is to a living creature, as petrified wood to a thriving branch. Other natural details accompany the dying trees—thorns, cacti, prickly desert growths, scourgelike leaves, and serpents. Title-page letters, Roman and angular, remain unvegetated and are never softened into natural Gothic. The vegetated flames of *Innocence* are now destructive and anticipate the wrath that will fall upon a corrupt society.

But though dead branch, scourgelike ivy, and jagged oak leaf are —or were—natural forms, Experience is not primarily a state of nature. It is psychological, political, social—a condition of man and his institutions, not of the universe. Analogous to the Fall that caused all nature to groan, capable of being symbolized by natural life in death and decay, Experience is the work of church, state, and man in society.

In *Experience*, Old Nobodaddy, his priests, and his kings have replaced Christ, Los, the Poet, and the Child—the gods of *Innocence*. The Urizen of *Experience* is not primarily the fallen Lucifer, the

---

[8] Cf. "Song," *Poetical Sketches, CW*, p. 7, a poem about sexual and mother-love among flowers, birds, and trees.

mythic figure of Blake's prophecy, but a social creature, a supporter of repressive institutions. The design to the poem that reverses the "The Divine Image" of *Innocence* ("The Human Abstract" of *Experience*) presents a bearded old man making nets that stand for established religion.

In Blake's angriest manifestations of him Urizen stands for the cruelty of an establishment that has failed to keep the peace and give the people bread and that has forced the young to work and weep in grime and suffering. The beautiful landscapes and borders of "Holy Thursday" are filled with corpses, one lying, ironically, on an oak leaf under the word "Holy," babes dead in a rich and fruitful land. The chimney sweeper's parents have gone to church to pray, leaving him to weep and work. His cry is matched by the sigh of a soldier that, surrealistically, flows as blood down a church wall, and by a broken old man, who appears in the design but not the text of "London," heading for his grave, an image of his god, Urizen, whose victim he is.

But institutional cruelty, though hideously direct in its results, is subtle in its means. The wily Urizen has transformed natural pity and love, the lovely daughters of the voice of God in *Innocence*, to institutional pity and charity in *Experience*. In an analysis of social "virtues" worthy of Bernard Mandeville, Blake perceives that Urizenic pity arises from social poverty, Urizenic mercy from a lack of equal happiness. Underneath the feet of Urizen grows a plant called Humility, which he waters with holy tears and holy fears. Such an institutionalized virtue finds the natural selfishness of the child intolerable; for healthy egotism might destroy obedience and obsequiousness—that miasma spread by the "Creeping Jesus,"[9] himself a ghastly perversion of the golden Lion-Christ of *Innocence*. When a Urizenic priest encounters an unspoiled boy who loves the little bird as much as he loves his father and who loves himself more than he loves his brother, the priest screams "What a fiend is here" and burns the child as a heretic. In *Experience* the unselfish clod that permits itself to be trodden under the feet of the cattle must be considered Urizenic[10]—on the side of that God and priest and

[9] "The Everlasting Gospel," Draft *d*, l. 59, *CW*, p. 752. See also Draft *c*, l. 25, *CW*, p. 750, and Letter to Cumberland, April 12, 1827, *CW*, p. 878.

[10] The Eternals call Urizen "a clod of clay" (*Urizen*, Plate 6, stanza 11, *CW*, p. 226). The Clod's philosophy that "builds a Heaven in Hell's despair" is parallel to that of the God of the Establishment and "his Priest & King,/Who make up a heaven of

king who make a heaven out of the chimney sweeper's misery. The *selfish* pebble of the brook sings a song the poet calls "meet."

One might suppose that to have thickened the clear water of Innocent mercy to the ooze of Established pity was Urizen's greatest achievement. But the amount of space Blake devotes to the suppression of natural sexuality suggests that this is in fact the ultimate perversion. The borders hint at repressed desire and its evil results. A blighted tree stands for envy, a sure result of repression by the father of jealousy; briars are the metaphoric weapons of repressive priests; the thistles and thorns of the desert represent chastity. Even the prophetic voice of the Bard-Christ, which sounds out only once, cannot be answered save by outcries against sexual frustration by Earth, a daughter of Albion chained by Urizenic jealousy. The nurse of Experience turns green with jealousy at the whispers of sex in the dale and laments the hypocritical disguises of adult life. The virgin either languishes and dreams of Los's sweet golden clime, or arms herself with the shield and spear of negation that drives the angel of love from her door. Sometimes the oppressor is a victim rather than an embodiment of Urizen—like the father in "A Little Girl Lost," who is not so much angered as frightened by his daughter's love. Even then the result is no less cruel—the banishment of daylight love for nighttime deceit, the repression and perversion of the young into the gray and palsied sufferings of the old.

It is always the institutional Urizen who perverts natural life. In the garden of love in *Experience* stands an altar, and priests read commands from a book on a lectern.

Blake's lament over lost love receives its most consummate expression in "The Sick Rose" (Plate XLVII). The worm, a male blight that destroys the flower, is the merry sparrow of *Innocence* transformed. The flower, an inversion of the aspiring growths of *Innocence*, falls, under a shower of Urizenic poison, ingloriously to the ground, a round, un-Gothic ball. Where the worm enters, a female joy flies away, as thorny stems and yellow, jagged leaves form arches that support languishing maidens. This is the land of

---

our misery" ("The Chimney Sweeper," *Songs of Experience, CW*, p. 212). For a full defense of this unorthodox interpretation, see my essay in the *Festschrift* to Alan D. McKillop (*Restoration and Eighteenth–Century Literature*, ed. Carroll Camden [Chicago, 1963]).

sorrow, the grave-plot of love from which Thel flees with a shriek.

Although the reader of Blake's words alone will find much to satisfy him in the social anger and human pathos of the verse, the student of Blake's composite art must rate the *Songs of Experience* slightly below the *Songs of Innocence*. In *Experience* Blake too often depended on his most elemental form—the simple illustration, in which bottom, top, or middle designs reproduce the scene or point the moral. Of true illumination as we have defined it, we have only one authentic example, "The Sick Rose." Only there does Blake approach the triumphant mastery of his most complex form that he revealed three times in the *Songs of Innocence*—in "Infant Joy," "The Divine Image," and "The Blossom." Occasionally in *Experience* the design and scene, embellished in rich and glowing color, belie the desired effect: dead bodies lie among rich blues and purples that almost reconcile us to the social disasters. In the most famous of all the Songs, the magnificent verbal "Tyger" is unworthily illustrated by a simpering animal.

In spite of these lapses from a standard Blake himself has set, the *Songs of Experience* does rival *Innocence* as his greatest work of composite art. Experience is, like Innocence, a serious and integrated idea. It is expressed by the pervasive metaphor of the Fall and of the expulsion from Eden that is recalled vividly on the title page and with subtle indirection elsewhere. Aesthetically, the volume breaks new ground. Weak in illumination, it brings a new refinement to what we have called decoration. In the "Introduction," "Earth's Answer," and "The Fly" Urizenic blue forms an appropriate background and the clouds superimposed on it constitute the successive stanzas—a form beautiful in itself and animated by its obvious relevance to the dying dispensation of the god of this nocturnal world. Even illustration is occasionally combined with decoration to form a page that approaches the integrated beauty of "The Sick Rose." In "Holy Thursday" the text is related to the top and bottom landscape by freely flowing lines formed by the dead tree and by the barren rocks. In "A Poison Tree" (Plate XLVI), Urizenic blue (the color is called "poisonous" in *Jerusalem*), the bare tree of institutional mystery, the baleful landscape, the dead body disposed in a cruciform shape on the ground like a Gothic tomb effigy—all these visual details support the indictment of Urizen-land. One of its citizens represses anger in accord with the established code, nourishes it with deceit while his foe lives, and rejoices unhypocritically when the man is dead. Thus is Christ crucified afresh by the respectable frustrations and revenges of an inhibiting society.

NEITHER EXPERIENCE NOR INNOCENCE

In one kind of illustration Blake attempts to represent the allegorical personifications of the poetry. Sometimes he brings to headpiece, tailpiece, or border such visionary horrors as the bloodcurdling "Ghost of a Flea." But other visual personifications are gentle forms of sky-born blue, yellow, and pink, figures from Milton's *Comus* or Collins' "Ode to Evening" come alive. Such creatures animate *The Book of Thel*, a successful example of the kind of illustration that reduplicates and reinforces the allegorical scenery of the verse.

Thel is an immortal virgin, lovely but unhappy, who dwells in what some critics consider the land of seed and embryo, and others, the Happy Valley of *Rasselas*, a languid Eden divorced from life. But small hints[11] in text and design suggest that Thel dwells among the daughters of Memory, that is, among the unvisionary classical or neoclassical pagans. Tired of the silvery Vergilian beauty of her life—of its limitations and its evanescence—she longs for the golden permanence of an Eden in which she can "hear the voice of him that walketh in the garden in the evening time." Full of that hope, but with a numbing sense that all else fades, she encounters the Lilly of

[11] The first engraved plate clearly makes Thel a daughter of "Mne (not "the") Seraphim." *Mne* recalls *Mnetha*, the mother of Har and Heva, who dwells in the vales of Har, whence Thel comes and to which she returns (*Tiriel* sec. 2, *Thel* iii. 10, iv. 22, *CW*, pp. 100, 129, 130). *Mne* and *Mnetha* both suggest the Greek word for memory, *Mnemosyne*. Blake later wrote that "the Greek Muses are *daughters of Mnemosyne* [Thel is a *daughter of Mne* Seraphim], or Memory, and not of Inspiration or Imagination" ("A Descriptive Catalogue," *CW*, pp. 565–66). In the "New Age" the "Daughters of Memory shall become the Daughters of Inspiration" (Preface to *Milton, CW*, p. 480). See also *CW*, pp. 496, 522, 525, 533, 783. The daughters of Mnemosyne, therefore, regularly symbolized classical culture and all its attendant and related evils and limitations. Thel seems to be one of them. She comes from the valley of Har in *Tiriel*—a poem full of classical reminiscences. As Miss Raine has seen, the plot of that poem is based on *Oedipus Coloneus*, and some of the descriptions recall Aeschylus. Tiriel (in the British Museum designs) wears a classical cloak, and Hela's garb suggests the kind of Greek garment Blake had copied from Greek vases. See "Some Sources of *Tiriel*," *Huntington Library Quarterly*, XXI (November, 1957), 9, 11, 12.

the Valley, the first of several natural beings who invite her to enter their world where a natural and uninhibited life is impregnated with the spirit of humble service and the presence of Christ the Lamb. Thel learns that the delicate Lilly enjoys the butterfly that bends her blossom, the lamb that crops her flowers, and all the humble, holy things that surround her. She also learns that the Cloud dies with the dew but rises again diurnally, and that the Clod of Clay loves the lowly worm in melting maternal affection. Thel is attracted by such a world, unknown to the Daughters of Memory, for this is a world of imaginative vision in which the humblest being loves and is tenderly loved, serves and is graciously served, and in which all that lives is holy. Thel is granted permission to enter it; but she sees, not the world of Innocence so attractively described by its humblest inhabitants, but the world of Experience—that is, the world of nature and love perverted into social repression. She sees her own grave—surely a symbol of sexual experience in a corrupt world—and the twisting roots of fallen nature. She hears a voice of sorrow from the ground that speaks of courtier-sex, of mercenary flattery, of lying and dark deceit, and of the impediments to joy that even nature now seems to impose. With a shriek Thel flees back to the land of languid frustration she had left.

The Book of Thel, like most of Blake's illuminations, opens with a title page. Thel, a daughter of Memory and not of Inspiration who dwells in a place of arrested development, appears a Theocritean or Vergilian shepherdess, Attic in profile, classical in dress, as well as Greek in name. She resembles the world of limited classical beauty Blake knew so well from the work of his friends Cumberland and Flaxman, of whose delicate line-figures she reminds us. Thel stands under a tree, whose shape and whose tiny buds form one of Blake's firmest symbols of Innocence becoming Experience (Plate XLVIII). It joins its symbolic force to that of the sky washes and of the male and female who emerge from the hearts of the flowers in a love embrace that betokens both the Edenic free love Thel is to witness and the perversion of love in Experience. The text itself begins with one of Blake's simplest forms of illustration—the headpiece that surrounds a short title. Once more, as on the title page, the water-color washes support the mood and tone, and the embracing mother and child and the nude male, bearing what may be regarded as a sexual symbol, alert us to the presence of natural love in the world

Thel is about to examine. Next, the delicate Lilly of the Valley bows low before Thel and enforces the theme of lowly service we have already noted. Next, another simple headpiece shows the worm on its lowly bed, and the Cloud—called a little Cloud in the poem but now seen as an adult male fully capable of wooing the dew—flies away to the amorous activity only very chastely alluded to in the poem. Next, Thel bows before a nativity in the world of Innocence; and as she imitates the courtesy of the Lilly, we know now that she is willing to leave the world of frustration she has known for the world of lowly service and joy. Observe that Blake's Mother Nature, the Clod of Clay, is an attractive young woman with the golden hair Blake always gives to his agents of salvation. The final page (Plate XLIXB), with its illustration fittingly at the bottom, provides a visual motif Blake will use again in *America*, innocent children riding a serpent—a motif perhaps deriving from an ancient Priapian design[12] (Plate XLIXA; see also Plate XXXC). In the world of Innocence Thel wishes to enter, sex is natural and can be mastered by even the fairest and the tenderest.

Of the three realms implied or described in the text—Thel's own world of frustration and inchoateness, the innocent world of natural joy, and the world of Urizenic perversion from which the shrieking Thel flees at the end—the designs, except for one or two details on the title page, are concerned only with Innocence, the land of the Lilly, the Worm, the Cloud, and the Clod. And within that world the designs emphasize the attractiveness of natural love. This two-fold concentration—first upon Innocence alone and then within Innocence upon its unperverted sexuality—sharpens the meaning of the poem. The virgin Thel flees from her own world because it *thwarts* natural desire, but she flees back to it when she sees the greater evil of a society that *perverts* natural desire. Better to be a Theocritean shepherd than a prostitute, better a languishing Corydon than a leering courtier.

Some of the *Songs of Innocence and Experience* exemplify Blake's simplest way of uniting the arts in illustration, when design merely reduplicates the natural scene described or alluded to in the text.

---

12 The sexual implications of Blake's design are clear. They are even clearer if its source is Priapian: a cupid riding on a phallus in a design from Herculaneum reproduced in *Le Antichità di Ercolano Esposte* (Naples, 1757———), Vol. VI, Plate 94 (see Plate XLIXA).

The Book of Thel is a masterpiece of somewhat greater complexity, in which the design represents and reinforces the allegorical landscape of the poem. But even it must yield in aesthetic richness to those more ambitious and complex examples of illumination, "The Sick Rose" of *Experience* and the three flame-flower pages of *Innocence*.

CHAPTER VII

Revolutionary Art

Always an adaptable artist—now using lyrical, now prophetic lines, now suiting the sound to "terrific" sense, now to prosaic [1]—Blake did not allow his visual-verbal language to harden. Although he never really surpassed the satisfying unity of what we have called illumination, he continued restlessly to work on freer, more flexible forms. Most of his pages testify to the continuing fertility of his invention. But a few striking failures [2] testify also to the enormous difficulties of Blake's task: trying to speak an apocalyptic word in a new form to a generation that would not hear; trying to express an original vision without the corrective benefits of a sympathetic or critical audience.

Many of Blake's most characteristic achievements as poet-painter are present in the Lambeth prophecies: the illustration of natural or allegorical descriptions and of metaphors, the use of counterpoint or contrast between word and design, the allegorical use of border motifs. At the same time Blake ventures upon new ways of relating the various elements of the form. A threefold division of the pages into illustration, decoration, and illumination is no longer possible, since the various kinds are now freely and boldly combined. Borders vary so enormously in size and shape,

[1] "Every word and every letter is studied and put into its fit place; the terrific numbers are reserved for the terrific parts, the mild & gentle for the mild & gentle parts, and the prosaic for inferior parts; all are necessary to each other" ("To the Public," *Jerusalem* I. iii, *CW*, p. 621).

[2] Blake did not usually fail in the way even some of his friendliest and ablest critics have supposed. S. Foster Damon believed that in *America* and other prophecies Blake said one thing in the language and something quite "detached" and independent in the design (*William Blake: His Philosophy and Symbols* [New York, 1924], pp. 332, 339). This heterodoxy is venerable: in the copy of *Europe* now in the British Museum, George Cumberland (I owe this identification to Mr. Bentley) has added passages from Milton, Shakespeare, Dryden, Rowe, Fletcher, and Mrs. Radcliffe, presumably to show what Blake really had in mind. In most of Blake's prophecies, however, the design can be explained within the confines of the poem—usually on the same page, sometimes on the contiguous pages, occasionally on remoter pages.

sometimes even dwarfing the text, that they can scarcely be called borders. Mythic figures do not remain in the landscape prepared for them, but fly to all corners of the page and, in the manner of baroque art, ignore the boundaries. Blake had always been, by contrast with his predecessors, an audacious designer of pages, but now he outdoes even himself. The medieval miniaturist and the emblematist are swallowed up by the mannerist follower of Goltzius and the friend of Fuseli. But as eccentricities multiply, one's interest does not decrease, and great enjoyment and profit reward concentrated and trained attention.

HEAVEN AND HELL

Blake's perverse and powerful recommendation of hellish energy arose from his own psychological depths. He defended artists against Reynolds' slander that they were tame and conventional,[3] and he always liked the morally adventurous, the gay, the wild better than those who count and think. "Mark! Active Evil is better than Passive Good."[4] He is supposed to have believed in a community of wives and to have said that he himself had committed many murders in the course of his life. In annotating Boyd's translation of Dante he wrote that "the grandest Poetry is Immoral, the grandest characters Wicked. . . . the Poet is Independent & Wicked; the Philosopher is Dependent & Good."[5]

Blake had a Byronic side, but to see him as a conventionally unconventional Satanist or a poseur in meretricious Romantic Agony is to insult his moral earnestness and revolutionary fervor. That fervor led him to break with Swedenborg, to whom he had been attracted. *The Marriage of Heaven and Hell* is not primarily the scorn of a libertine for a Puritan nor even of a free man for a predestinarian, but of a revolutionary for a timid accepter of existing order. Swedenborg's ethics were no more suited to the burning need for action than were the conventional pieties. "Prayers plow not! Praises reap not!"[6]

[3] "Painters are noted for being Dissipated & Wild." Annotations to Reynolds, *CW*, p. 454.

[4] Annotations to Lavater, *CW*, p. 77.

[5] Crabb Robinson, "Reminiscences," etc., in Arthur Symons, *Blake* (London, 1907), pp. 269, 270, 303–4; *Times Literary Supplement*, May 3, 1957, p. 277; *CW*, p. 412.

[6] *Marriage* ix. 20, *CW*, p. 152.

"Did he who made the Lamb make thee?" Blake's answer is now an exulting Yes. For in a revolutionary epoch the tiger of wrath is better than the horse of instruction, and Christ reveals himself more appropriately in the Leviathan and the tiger, who have "all the fury of a spiritual existence,"[7] than in the loving life of Innocence. Before the sapphire-studded consummation of *Jerusalem* can be attained, Los must transform the soft affections to cruelty and must work as "an inspired fury," a horror and an astonishment to all who see him.[8]

Blake had read the biblical prophets well. Before the final Rapture comes Armageddon, before Adam returns to Paradise comes the "dominion of Edom"—that kingdom south of Judah inhabited by the descendants of Esau, which in the Bible is the site of Armageddon, the final apocalyptic battle when Christ at his return destroys the empires of Gentile world. Blake refers us in the *Marriage* to the thirty-fourth and thirty-fifth chapters of Isaiah's prophecy. The second of these describes final bliss, when the lion and lamb lie down together in a desert that blossoms as a rose. The first describes the great and terrible day of the Lord, when his indignation is visited upon the nations and when the palace of the nobleman becomes a court for vultures, dragons, and screech owls. Blake in the *Marriage* recruits for the army of Armageddon. When Rintrah roars and shakes his fire, the just man, who was formerly meek, "rages in the wild / Where lions roam." Now the sneaking serpent—the priest and king of the Establishment—has pre-empted the old virtue and "walks / In mild humility." He can be destroyed only if the lamb becomes a lion, if the good man adopts the tiger's destructive wrath.[9]

But though the *Marriage* calls for a revolutionary ethic, it also celebrates those qualities in human life and art that both serve and transcend the social need—the lover's and the artist's passion. The artist's improvement of sensual gratification through the cleansing of perception and the lover's unabashed cultivation of exuberant bodily instincts are revolutionary energies that can expunge conventional evil. But they can also lay bare the infinite purposes of life and nature and provide the blueprint of paradise.

[7] *CW*, p. 156.
[8] *Jerusalem* I. viii. 17–18, I. ix. 26–27, I. x. 22, *CW*, pp. 627, 628, 629.
[9] *CW*, pp. 148–49.

Some copies of *The Marriage of Heaven and Hell* are as beautiful as anything Blake's pen, pencil, graver, brush, and acid bath ever produced. His words alternate between gnomic aphorism and grotesque, allegorical description. His designs consist mostly of headpieces and tailpieces and of very freely rendered borders—so unconventional, in fact, that they cease to be borders and run like little decorative trickles between the lines and even the words of the text. As composite art, the work is highly coherent. The designs, in Blake's best manner, reinforce and interpret, and do not merely repeat, the textual motifs.

Blake's philosophy leaves room for reason as the circumference that bounds energy, and he foresees a time when it will unite with the instinctual side to produce the perfect man in a perfect society. But the marriage envisioned in this work is neither so remote nor so prudential as that. The title page (Plate L)—a fine work of iconographic art that summarizes the ensuing action and gives it the proper rhetorical emphasis—shows three things: (1) that on earth Urizenic experience still reigns (trees are bare, their branches form Roman shapes, and men are desolate), (2) that redemptive energies, sweeping up to the surface in a baroque diagonal, arise from below the earth, traditionally the seat of hell, and (3) that the cause of this upward movement is the love embrace of two young nudes—a demon from the fire on the left and an angel from the earth on the right. That embrace is not to be interpreted as an ultimate ontological union of psychological opposites, but as the birth of revolutionary action. The conventional angel, who stretches out his arms to embrace the hellish demon, will be completely destroyed and will rise as Elijah, who ascended into heaven in a fiery chariot and was, in traditional symbology, a precursor of the returning Christ.

The pages that follow all praise the hellish wisdom of energy and deride the conventional unwisdom of institutional reason and piety. The designs now and then recall *Innocence*—as if to remind us, through scenes like the one in which a boy hands grapes to a bare-bosomed girl, that one of the chief ingredients of that lovely state was natural love (see Plate XXXV). More often the designs (Urizenic loops, snakes, crouched bodies) symbolize Experience, the state of man and nature under Urizenic blight, and establish a contrast with the words that praise art, love, instinct, revolt, and energy. The most striking visual polarity is reserved for the end, a unit consisting of the four concluding plates of the *Marriage* proper. The headpiece of the twenty-first page (Plate LIA) shows Blake's Poetic Man rising to newness of life, the ultimate accomplishment of the cleansing hellish fires. The tailpiece of the last page (Plate LIB; see also Plates XVI, XLIA) provides a striking contrast—Nebuchadnezzar eating grass, or man reduced to animality by that blighting god Urizen, whose face the face of the crawling king unmistakably recalls.

ALBION'S DAUGHTERS

The *Visions of the Daughters of Albion*—if it bears other political meaning, the key has been lost—is a ringing indictment of marital slavery and sexual repression. The slight narrative and the accompanying lamentations tell us that the lovely Oothoon committed an act of "Innocence," an act, that is, of love and poetic fancy. She flew to the beautiful vale of Leutha and picked a marigold, which she saw now as flower and now as nymph in the unimpeded twofold vision Blake's poets and seers always have. This act, which created joy in the flower and in the one who picked it, describes love between Oothoon and Theotormon—love that caused her husband, Bromion —a Urizenic tyrant who enslaves Africans and Americans abroad and women at home—to denounce her as a harlot and commit an act of marital rape. Neither Oothoon's act of joy nor her husband's act of anger breaks their bonds. Theotormon, whom Oothoon has loved, is a jealous ineffectual man, incapable of joining his beloved in her bold rejection of society's charge that she is a prostitute.

While the timid lover converses with the shadows of the past, the others bring the central issue to sharp focus. The angry Bromion preaches the gospel of Urizen that one law must govern all of life and that its claims must be enforced by whip and chain. Oothoon and her sisters plead the uniqueness of each joy, the infinite variety of life, the healthy blisses of Innocence, where "every thing that lives is holy."

The poem that preaches the gospel of *Innocence* lacks its exuberant borders. Technically the *Visions* resembles *The Book of Thel*, both in the beauty of its coloring (in the light delicate shades of earlier versions as well as in the rich blues, reds, and purples of later) and in the simple directness with which the designs portray the scene and characters of the action.

95

The frontispiece (Plate LII) is a visual analogue of the central situation. In a cave that the text calls a religious den built upon lust sits Oothoon, chained to her husband, the rapist, Bromion. The pair—called "adulterate,"[10] since by the purer standards of Innocence marriage cannot remove the sin of a loveless union—are placed back to back, female meekness linked to male terror, the condition of Urizenic sexual union. Bromion, bearded, Urizenic in countenance, opens his mouth in fear as though he foresees the end of his reign. The waters of jealousy[11] lap the floor of the cave, at whose mouth sits the lamenting Theotormon (beloved of Oothoon and of the other daughters), ineffectually bemused with the past. The sun is up, not in an apocalyptic sunrise but in the dawn of another day of fresh tears in the charnel house; it is a round staring Urizenic eye, with a lid that resembles a bat's or moth's wing, that steady symbol of the oppressing Establishment.

The letters of the title page (Plate LIIIA) are decorated, not with the organic life of Innocence, but with bodies in postures of grief, some obviously desperate and angry, Albion's oppressed daughters now in the enslaving night of Experience. In contrast a lovely rainbow crosses the title, a sign not of dawn but of the world of Innocence, Leutha's vale, where Oothoon plucked her flower. She is represented at the bottom of the design, fleeing in fear after her act, her flight and fear explained by the hovering figure of Urizen. Charged by Albion's daughters with being a "Mistaken Demon of Heaven" and the "Father of Jealousy," Urizen appears only here, his mouth open, his eyes staring, his flame-wings spread out.

Urizen in flight is imitated in the last design (Plate LIIIB) by Oothoon, who flies in the sky with an expression of grief on her face, as three of Albion's daughters sit on the rocky shore of the frontispiece and echo her wail. But though her arms are spread like Urizen's wings, Oothoon, unlike Bromion, is not the tyrant's agent but his victim, on whom he has set his stamp. He can affect her shape and form, but he cannot touch her mind, which remains free, bold, receptive.

In this prophecy Blake has recorded the laments of those who lack the lineaments of gratified desire. If, by an act of nature or

[10] *Visions* ii. 4, *CW*, p. 190.
[11] *Ibid.*, ii. 4: "black jealous waters."

protest, England's daughters achieve satisfaction, they pay the price of becoming social outcasts.

Blake lived in an epoch that was at least officially Christian. His mind was nourished by the fervent reading of the Books of Daniel and Revelation, of *Paradise Lost* and *Paradise Regained*, and his visual imagination was stirred by visions of the Last Days in Dürer, Michelangelo, Raphael, and Giulio. He must also have sensed some affiliation with the millennialism of seventeenth-century revolutionary dissent. It came natural to him to interpret his own turbulent times in terms of a Christian eschatology radically adapted to his purpose.

The eschatology of the dissenting groups has usually believed that the Day of the Wrath would be preceded by unspeakable corruption in human institutions and human life and that that corruption would be challenged sometime near the end of the present dispensation by an Elijah or a John the Baptist *redivivus*. In response to that challenge the established powers would unite under the banner of Satan, appearing as an Anti-Christ, a man of unanswerable power precisely because his evil so neatly reversed and parodied the good. Just as the forces of Anti-Christ were about to take over the earth and crush the prophets, Christ and his angels would return, triumph over his enemies at Armageddon, and inaugurate the millennial reign.

Blake, like his forerunners in the Year One Thousand and like countless Hebrews and Christians in ages of war and persecution, read the signs of his revolutionary times and of his waning century to mean that the end was near. An eccentric, unorthodox believer, but not a superstitious soothsayer, Blake endowed his apocalypticism with no literal belief in impossible natural wonders and primitive supernatural signs. And as a humane man with a sympathetic imagination, he could not attribute military cruelty to Christ and his servants. But Blake's revolutionary prophecies do possess elements of traditional apocalypticism. Living near the end of a century, born in a period of imperialistic wars, coming to maturity during the American Revolution and to the full bloom of his genius during the French Revolution, aware of impending economic change, and sick to the bone of ruling hypocrisy, he viewed the events of his own days

97

as the fulfillment of prophecy, as the culmination of cosmogonic myth. He also sensed, as earlier prophets had, that things would get worse before they got better—that night would be darkest just before dawn. It is in fact in the predawn dark that most of his prophecies begin. The Anti-Christ of the Lambeth books was William Pitt the younger, the precursor (Elijah or John) was the Poetic Genius, and the pre-Armageddon rally of counterrevolutionary forces was England's military preparation after the French regicide in 1793.[12]

Like his greatest predecessor, the author of the Book of Revelation, Blake told his story in a dark and grotesque allegory compounded of both universal and specific contemporary meanings. The eschatological mind unites the story of the universe and the story of the age, and in no classical work of prophecy can the two strains be disentangled. Blake's illuminated prophecies are no exception. But the proportions vary in each work—*Europe* is vastly more mythic than *America*—and it is the chief burden of the revolutionary works to arouse our desires for a better life, not to appease the appetite for harmony among the stars.

In *America*, one of Blake's greatest achievements in composite art, almost every visual detail receives support in the text. A new type of free, uninhibited border, composed of symbolic forms relevant to the message, ties part to part and includes within its large movement the main design that had sometimes been conceived of separately and that, even in a proximate work like the *Visions of the Daughters of Albion*, did not go much beyond textual illustration. Beside tying together elements on a single page, the everchanging border relates page to page and accompanies, with continuously but coherently changing symbolism, the drive of the words toward an apocalyptic climax.

In the frontispiece, which is a slight revision of an earlier painting entitled "Breach in the City—the Morning after Battle,"[13] Blake sets the time of his action and presents his *dramatis personae*. The large, winged creature, who sits in a wall already breached by the cannon of revolution that appears lower left, is either Albion's Angel (a personification of the Tory Establishment under George

---

[12] David Erdman, *Blake: Prophet against Empire* (Princeton, 1954), pp. 185–86.
[13] For a reproduction, see *Fogg Museum Bulletin*, Vol. X (November, 1943).

III, now shackled though not finally defeated) or the Poetic Genius in an age of arid classicism and aristocratic art. If the latter, as is more likely, he joins the sad woman, the clinging children, the dead, monstrous stones of the wall, the frowning clouds of the sky that resemble the wings and the wall to compose a static and frozen scene in the very heart of Urizen-land. In Blake's view the American war was the beginning of the end—its fires would light France to red fury—and it had in fact breached the wall of that Establishment which was now rising in counterrevolutionary resistance—an action that in the prophet's vision would prove to be its death gasp.

The letters of the title page are, alongside the letters of Innocence with their shoots of organic life, as lifeless as the stones and bodies of the frontispiece. An old man and a young woman at the top read Urizenic books, while children and youth vainly invite them to joy. At the bottom, in a symbol of that sexual repression Blake felt always accompanied political tyranny, a woman frantically kisses a lifeless male. On the first page of the Preludium (Plate LIVA), surely one of Blake's very greatest pages in the economy and suggestiveness of its symbols, the revolutionary protagonist of the poem, the fiery boy Orc, visited by the daughter of Urthona and by Los but still chained like Prometheus to a rock or like Christ to his cross, shows that the old repressive dispensation is not yet over. In a brilliant visual statement of cause and effect the roots of the dead tree of Experience (its branches form a round Urizenic arch) create a cave deep in the earth that houses a squatting Urizenic victim. On the second page of the Preludium Orc breaks through the surface of the earth, as the grape vine and the wheat of the left border shoot sprays upward and presage the final redemptive harvest. The revolutionist's rising from the ground uproots the Established tree and at the same time destroys the earth-caves of frustration and despair formed by its roots.

On the first page of the Prophecy proper, the design is lighter: lines curl, birds fly, creepers wind in and out of the text, and licking flames form borders left and center, flames that must stand for the revolutionary Orc, who on the next plate is described as "Intense, naked, a Human fire." The page (p. 4) containing that phrase shows, contrapuntally, the counterattack by Urizen, who shoots a pestilential arrow, and by his lieutenant, Albion's angel, here in the shape of a fire-breathing dragon, as oppressed humanity suffers on the earth below. The next plate (p. 5) presents the antagonists: at the top, young nude revolutionaries carry the scale and sword of justice, while at the bottom the serpent and evil men are cast into the flames of revolutionary destruction. The text and design are extremely close on the plate (p. 6) that contains a resurrection hymn and a parallel design showing a man, doubtless mankind, rising from his grave, looking heavenward, and recalling Christ. Left and right, leafy sprays presage a similar redemption of nature. The last words of this plate, "and now the Lion & Wolf shall cease," produce the illustration of the next (p. 7), a scene of Innocence which bears no relation to the text, but which, as always in Blake, at once recalls Eden and anticipates the new Jerusalem. Blake here expresses an Isaiah mood in which ram and child foretell the day when nations shall learn war no more. The true antagonist, the force behind Albion's Angel, Urizen himself, now appears (p. 8)— appropriately, since his presence in the design is justified by his presence in Orc's speech:

> The times are ended; shadows pass, the morning 'gins to break
> The fiery joy, that Urizen perverted to ten commands . . .
> That stony law I stamp to dust and scatter religion abroad
> To the four winds as a torn book, & none shall gather the leaves.

Vegetation had been present in *America*, but never before this plate (p. 9) has Blake allowed it to spread so generously across the page. Here the lines, whorls, and crosshatchings laugh at the tyrant's teeth-grinding complaint that he cannot smite the grain. The little babe, lying safe in the wheatfield, may stand for the "fatness of the earth" the tyrant is powerless to quench [14] (Plate LIVB). Next (p. 10) Orc rises in flames, not out of the earth as formerly. Nothing in the text supports the design, which seems to grow out of the line that begins the next page (p. 11), "Fiery the Angels rose." Boston's angel bitterly describes a society in which pity and generosity are a trade by which men grow rich—a speech accompanied, contrapuntally, by designs that recall the world of Innocence, where the young can master both the serpent of sex and the swan of the imagination. After the Innocence of this plate, comes the Experience of the next

[14] The color in some copies seems to imply that the babe is dead. If so, one must acknowledge that different copies can occasionally suggest diametrically opposite meanings.

(p. 12): oppressed man goes to his grave under the blasted tree that represents Urizenic society, down into the root and fungus whence Orc arose and whence redeemed man shall also rise. The reference in the text of the next page (p. 13) to the oppressor's awful wings justifies showing him at the top as a vulture tearing the flesh of Promethean man and at the bottom as a predatory fish doing the same thing.

In one of his subtlest metaphysical moments Blake next (p. 14) describes Albion's counterattack as a "blight that cuts the tender corn when it begins to appear" and devotes the entire illustration to this single metaphor, less than one line long: a woman whose loins encompass a serpent trains to submission ("blights") a boy ("the tender corn") under a tree with a cavelike opening—these along with the two large books on which his elbows rest, his hands clasped as if in prayer, constituting an ensemble of repressive symbols (Plate LVA). At the top left of the next plate (p. 15) bodies bend in submissive postures under the dead tree of oppression while at the bottom nude bodies rise in the revolutionary flames that will restore their natural energy and dignity by cleansing society. But the last plate (p. 16)—for thus does Blake usually tie beginning and end together—returns to the mood of the frontispiece (Plate LVB). The designs recall the status quo that provoked and justified revolutionary terror. The words tell how the defeated Urizen's tears fall from his leprous head into the Atlantic voids beneath; in the design the hair of a kneeling woman, his victim, falls down the side of the page like water. The branches of dead trees behind the weeping worshiper recall earlier border motifs and distantly suggest perverted human forms.

America begins and ends with powerful representations of ruling tyranny and its effect on humanity. In between come bold alternations of the dead, frustrating present and a fiery, redemptive future, as the frozen lines and forms of the opening melt into flame or revive into life. In a union of designs that are primary and a text that, though long and verbally brilliant, is inscriptive, Blake allows no one element to destroy the other. He uses all the resources at his disposal—moving line, verbal tableau, symbolic figure. With unabashed literalness he renders the fire that will soon consume, root and branch, the venerable Establishment, that is now in its last counterattack.

After *America*—the best of the Lambeth prophecies and one of Blake's greatest triumphs in composite art—*Europe* comes as an anticlimax, not because it lacks individual pages that are as brilliant as anything Blake ever did but because it lacks the total unity and inner coherence of the slightly earlier work. Some pages are energetic —compressed into intense meaning by a wonderful economy of means. Blake's mathematical deity, who applies his compasses to the globe in the frontispiece, recalls Blake's own representations of Newton, countless personifications of Mathematics, Architecture, and Learning in Western art, and the Ancient of Days in both the Old Testament and Milton. The frontispiece, which thus introduces the antagonist of the poetic action, anticipates some of the most important subsequent scenes: when Albion's Angel sees his master Urizen on the Atlantic void; when Newton, Urizen's greatest neoclassical creation, tries to frustrate change by blowing his counter-revolutionary trumpet; and when Urizen's brazen book of codified religion is copied by priests and kings over all the world.[15] The title page introduces the serpent which, next to Nobodaddy, is Blake's most cogent symbol of a naturalistic and rationalistic society (see Plate LXVIB). The huge serpent that coils from a snaky tree across and up the page, his head and neck dividing words of the title, is a unifying linear motif; but it also, along with the smaller snake that coils across the bottom, anticipates that brilliant passage in which Blake describes the serpent temples of the Druids, who closed the heavens to infinity, overwhelmed the five senses, hollowed the eyes to sightless orbs, made of God a tyrant—changing "the infinite to a serpent."[16]

The plate popularly called "Plague" is a brief and intense indictment of pious pity. A bellman stands indifferent by two suffering women near a churchdoor bearing the words "Lord Have Mercy Upon Us." Helpless official pity and desperate suffering are juxtaposed in a searing visual irony, parallel to the verbal description of Urizen as one who feeds his soul with pity while the youth of England "curse the pain'd heavens."[17]

Such pages alternate with brilliant revolutionary cartoons, in which appear Burke, Pitt, George III, and possibly the Archbishop

[15] *Europe* xiv. 33, xi. 1–5, xiii. 5, *CW*, pp. 244, 242, 243.
[16] *Ibid.*, x. 16–23, *CW*, p. 241.
[17] *Ibid.*, xii. 4–5, *CW*, p. 242.

of Paris (Plate III). Both the universal symbols and the cryptic cartoons (impossible to interpret without a detailed knowledge of the frightened counterrevolutionary moves of the English government in 1793) are often syncopated with the text, to set up a cross-rhythm between the old (expressed in the illustrations) and the new (expressed by the trumpet calls of the words). The designs, though powerful, do not bear away all the aesthetic honors. The impish song of the fairy that introduces the poem, the lovely adaptation of Milton's *Nativity Ode* that creates a Christlike harmony amid the strident Urizenic discord, the sharply ironic praise of female dominion, and the brilliantly analytical description of Druidic culture are among Blake's best pages of prophetic verse.

CHAPTER VIII

Prophecies Major and Minor

A prophet is not a sensational predicter of things to come but a seer into the life of men and nations who knows how to tell historic time. He interprets man's destiny in terms of his past, and he either summons men to action or exhorts them to patience, because, as one who sees spiritual causes behind temporal effects, he knows when the fulness of time has come.[1]

An apocalyptic point of view and a prophetic manner of expression came to Blake early and easily. Even as a youth he saw nations as clouds and political events as comets that make the night red. Societies were sick with a dead man's pallor seen by the flickering light of a taper, stars trembled, a scroll symbolized fate and terror, God drew his arrows, and the poet, like Isaiah, cried out, "Who can stand?"[2] Blake was a lifelong student of the Bible, first in translation and then also in its original tongues and in the interpretations of Milton, Raphael, Dürer, Michelangelo, and Giulio Romano. In criticism he adhered fervently to the growing school that preferred the sublimity of Genesis to the drawing-room beauty of Pope, and as a writer he was inspired by what he believed with all his being was the authentic and inescapable word of God.

URIZEN

In the minor prophecies—the books of *Urizen*, *Los*, and *Ahania* —the two most important figures are Urizen and Los. In these earlier myths Urizen is incomparably the more interesting, for

---

[1] "Prophets, in the modern sense of the word, have never existed. Jonah was no prophet in the modern sense, for his prophecy of Nineveh failed. Every honest man is a Prophet; he utters his opinion both of private & public matters ... A Prophet is a Seer, not an Arbitrary Dictator" (Annotations to Watson, *CW*, p. 392).

[2] *CW*, pp. 12, 30, 31, 33, 34.

Blake, like Milton, made his Satan more palpable and persuasive than his God. It is difficult to find a time when Urizen, as either an embryonic or a completely formed symbol, was not present in Blake's imagination. Adumbrated in the seventies, formulated as a concept in the eighties, and fully visualized from the early nineties on, Urizen is, though unpleasant, solid and inescapable. In the juvenilia his icy repressions and hoary conventions are anticipated in Winter, who carries a scepter and rides an iron car, in the old men who are given over to weary contemplation, and in those mad creatures who hate and fear the morning light. Urizen almost springs full-blown in that inept allegory of Pride, who leads a revolt against his father, Reason, and "tear(s) him from his throne"[3] as torrents roll down his white beard. By 1788—the year of his first engraved stereotypes, which contain a faint but precise delineation of the old man—Blake had defined cosmic evil as a void in space, and personal vice as "whatever is Negative"—"the omission of act in self & the hindering of act in another." On Lavater's sentence (that the believer in an impersonal god falls into "an immense abyss that first absorbs his powers, and next himself") Blake commented, "most superlatively beautiful & most affectionately Holy and pure." That insight of 1788 underlay *The Book of Urizen* (1794), in which Blake describes the origin of evil as the creation of a "soul-shudd'ring vacuum," an "abominable void"—an "unknown, abstracted, brooding, secret" power of dark negation.

Urizen has Greek, Roman, and Hebrew as well as English blood in his veins. His name and function recall the Greek verb ὁρίζειν (*orizein*, to define, or make boundaries), and his face recalls classical statues of sightless, bearded, warlike men and the God of the Old Testament as portrayed by countless painters of the Western school. A sun deity in his prelapsarian state, according to Blake's later myth, he may be related to Saturn, who was sometimes represented with huge right leg drawn up, holding a serpent that bites his tail, a large sickle resting beside him—a classical figure

[3] "Then She Bore Pale Desire," *CW*, p. 42. Compare this action with one represented in *Milton* (*CW*, p. 497; Huntington copy, Plate 15): Milton the liberator strides up to the figure of Urizen, seated as if on a throne and partly supporting himself by his arms on the tablets of the law. The poet seizes the hoary tyrant by the shoulders as if to dethrone him—an action that causes rejoicing in the heavens above.

Other references in this paragraph come from *CW*, pp. 2–3, 8–9, 82, 88, 222.

whom the mythologist of Blake's age equated with Noah.[4] He may also—for he struggles in the waters of materialism[5]—be related to the classical Neptune, whose beard flows like water or ice from his nose and whose face has some of the stubborn blankness of Blake's great negation (Plate XLA), or to the sightless and bearded faces of saints frozen into cruel conventionality by the established church (Plate LVI).

Urizen conveys powerful satiric meaning because the traces in his lineaments of traditional dignity suggest that the cruelty, ignorance, and repression he represents are perversions of the good (see Plates XLIIB, LIII, LXXIII). Books are good but Urizen has made them legal tablets. Religion, which is created by the imagination and can create the glorious freedom of the sons of God, Urizen has transformed into the whips and wheels of church and state.

The minor prophecies add many vivid details, verbal and visual, to the portrait of the institutional Urizen. As a primeval priest, with the tablets of the law at his back as though they were his own stony wings, he squats on a book bearing a mystical letter (Plate I). Tears of pious and conventional pity ooze from his compressed lids and drop into his ropy frozen beard (Plate LVIIA). Dividing, partitioning, dropping the plummet line, he is an architect of the skeletal abstractions he calls science. The enemy of gratified desire, he smites his passionate son Fuzon with Sinaitic poison and nails his corpse to the institutional tree of mystery, as nerves of joy melt and the drying senses rush inward.[6]

Urizen is also a natural force—winter, storm, snow, ice, water, rock, sand, death itself. He lies in a desolate landscape as his hand rests on a skull (Plate VI). He sits as a skeleton without flesh in the fire, he struggles in water, he emerges from a green vegetable cave,

---

[4] Andrew Tooke, *The Pantheon* (London, 1783), pp. 137, 144. Blake's Urizen resembles the sightless and bearded face of John the Baptist's severed head in William Stukeley, *Palaeographia Britannica* (London, 1743), Plate V—an engraving of an "ancient Altar in Alabaster" dedicated to St. John (Plate LVI). Blake's own representations of Urizen or Urizenic figures who are either his surrogates or victims are too numerous to mention. The suggestion made above (p. 105) that the early personification of Winter in the *Poetical Sketches* adumbrates Urizen receives some support in Blake's illustrations of Cowper's "Winter": an old man like Urizen holds a bare, leafless, small tree in one hand (Geoffrey Keynes, *The Tempera Paintings of William Blake* [London, 1951], Plate II).

[5] *Urizen*, Plate 6.

[6] *Ibid.*, Plates 1, 13, 21; *The Book of Ahania*, chaps. ii–iv.

he sits under blasted trees with the poisonous serpent, he weaves a frosty net. He is Blake's symbol of Newtonian nature—cold. remote, mathematical, empty.[7]

LOS

There are good old men in Blake—some of them patriarchs, some of them prophets. Without these to serve as standards, how could the perversions of Urizen be measured? There are also evil young men—Satan and Rintrah in chain mail, for example. But during Blake's early and middle career, heroes were usually young and villains old, for he persisted in seeing life with the immodest and impudent eyes of youth. In Blake's Trinity (Christ, Los, and Orc) the Father is the Son, the Son is a young Artist, and Holy Ghost is a revolutionary, not a comforter—all in the full flower of uninhibited manhood.

Urizen began as a personification of Winter riding a northern car. Los began as Spring with dewy locks who arouses a love-sick land, as the prince of love who rides a flaming car, as the Golden Apollo who brings the light of truth from "Sol's palace high," as the melancholy, dreaming "I" of the lyrics, and as the young Morning who shakes his curly, golden locks (see Plate XXVIIA). In *Innocence* Los appears as the Christ who brings safety, as the shepherd who tends the sheep, as the poet who walks into the future and sings his song, and as the child on the cloud who is the subject of vision. He will appear again in the major prophecies as the keeper of the artistic flame in Reason's darkest night.[8]

Since Blake's thought could not escape the cycle of Unity-Fall-Restoration that has dominated thought from Moses to Freud, Los must fall in order to rise. We see him falling and fallen in Blake's vivid and energetic baroque—plunging down in flames, howling, suffering, rolled up into a fetal shape, and at work with hammer and tongs (Plate LVIIB; cf. Plate LX). A void being intolerable, Los

---

[7] *Urizen*, Plates 4, 5, 6, 8, 13, 27; *The Song of Los*, title page. Blake could treat his Death-God with comic contempt as Nobodaddy—an anagram for Nobody's Daddy (*CW*, p. 185). But the scurrilous verses about the belching and coughing old man are not matched in the designs or even in the canonical engraved works. There Urizen is a solid, solemn symbol of dark power—sometimes as universal as Satan, sometimes as particular as George III; sometimes as pervasive as Winter, sometimes as individual as an archbishop.

[8] *CW*, pp. 1, 6, 8, 9, 14, 15, 21, 36, 37; see above, pp. 77, 79 and below, pp. 117–18.

must give to Urizenic nothing a local habitation and a name. Out of the evil and empty abyss that Urizen had formed in the center of things Los must extract a material fuel that can be burned on the Last Day.[9] He must shape the Great Indefinite into forms that can be isolated and destroyed.

Urizen before Los (Blake) is a nameless, shapeless force poisonously insinuated into our holiest institutions. Urizen after Los (Blake) is a palpable reality that can be cast out of life to its purification and redemption.

Los not only creates a body for evil; he also produces the destroyer of evil (the red Orc, the spirit of revolution) and the mother of Orc, Enitharmon, Los's emanation, whose separation from his side causes frightful pain, since primal unity does not suffer division gladly. The mother of Orc is also the creator of Beulah, Blake's moony land of the love of the sexes, the only kind of love possible in the dispensation of Urizen's blue night and stars. Although sexual love can be perverted into either frustrated marriage or dark prostitution, it is the clearest augury of innocence we possess, a producer of sweet joy early in life and of redemptive energy. Enitharmon and Los create the love of the clod for the child, of the dew for the cloud, of the child for the lamb, and of Oothoon for Leutha's flower. But, in the perspective of the minor prophecies and the revolutionary epics, the creation of Innocence, however lovely, is transcended by the creation of Orc; in that creative act Los, an Apollo become Prometheus, brings down destructive and redemptive fire.[10]

The minor prophecies tell in picture and word the story of the past (Eden, the Fall) and of the present (the dispensation of Urizen from Egypt to the France of Louis XVI) in order to nerve man for Armageddon and assure him of the new Eden. At their worst these works are visionary cartoons with private and undecipherable meanings, and Blake is a Gillray of the infinite. At their best they provide unforgettable images of individual good and institutional evil—images Blake will use again in *Milton* and *Jerusalem*, his visions of redeemed reality.

[9] *Urizen*, Plates 9, 14, 16, 17, 18; *The Book of Los* ii. 5–9.
[10] *Urizen*, chaps. v–vii; Northrop Frye, *Fearful Symmetry* (Princeton, 1947), esp. chaps. vii, viii.

Blake's two Christian epics are united by profound resemblances of subject and style. Both derive—directly in *Milton*, indirectly in *Jerusalem*—from Blake's three-year slumber by the sea at Felpham, and both are hewn out of that spectacular literary ruin, *The Four Zoas*,[11] which looks back to the revolutionary books and ahead to the major prophecies. These two works present both sides of Blake's famous equation, that religious prophecy and imaginative art are one and the same. *Milton* embodies the artistic, *Jerusalem* the religious side; and the two complementary prophecies together say that without the prophetic message the poet becomes Satan's laureate and that without imagination religion becomes the Abomination of Desolation (that is, the quintessential evil of hypocrisy—noble ideals compromised by involvement in the state). Both works, though they take account of the unloosing of Orc and of the passage of mankind through a Great Tribulation leading to Armageddon, yoke the revolutionary spirit to Christian love and sacrifice. For both epics spring from their author's renewed commitment to an undogmatic Christianity that is compounded of medieval and mystical charity and of the spirit of English dissent. Blake made Madame Guion and St. Teresa, Milton and the Hervey who wrote the pious meditations, the proclaimers of the Everlasting Gospel. Monk, Methodist, and Blake, united in the bonds of an undogmatic, antinomian, and humane emphasis upon love, attack the warlike Christianity of Paul, Constantine, Luther, Charlemagne, and Pitt's Establishment.

Technically and aesthetically, the two major prophecies are strikingly alike. Their pages now and then recall *Innocence* but more often embody the dead forms of *Experience*. The long septenary line of verse often pre-empts the space and reduces the border to a thin unimpressive line. In both works the narrative is interrupted by full pages of design, and both make generous use of top, bottom, and middle illustrations. Often the mighty message seems too potent for the form and seems to impel the designer to attempt the visually impossible. For all the splendor of solitary pages and for all the power of their total effect, both *Milton* and

---

[11] See G. E. Bentley, Jr., "The Failure of Blake's *Four Zoas*," *Texas Studies in English*, XXXVII (1958), 102–13.

Jerusalem are—if they are too rigorously considered—failures as composite art. The textless thirty-eighth plate of *Milton*, with hovering eagle and embracing couple, seems best explained by the ninety-fourth plate of *Jerusalem*, and on other magnificently designed and excitingly surrealist pages the swan blowing bubbles in the water, the gaudily bedecked woman swimming, and the man with the head of a bird remain either unaccounted for or only opaquely interpreted by the text.[12]

But though *Milton* and *Jerusalem* are brothers, they are not twins. Both make of the once mighty Urizen a minor figure, but each makes its own kind of substitution. *Milton* replaces the cruel-holy representative of the venerable Church-State with Satan, who shifts the emphasis to the evils of materialistic philosophy and natural religion. In *Jerusalem* old Nobodaddy's place has been taken by Rahab-Vala, the Virgin Harlot, the mother of War and Mystery. In *Jerusalem*, though Tyburn's tree, the neighbourhood at Lambeth, Scofield, and Hayley are present and though everything begins and ends on Albion's druidic rocky shore, the landscapes of the old and new Jerusalem are even more prominent, making the vision universal in time and place. In *Milton* the hero and heroine cut paths from Great Eternity through the trackless wastes of chaos into the blue mundane shell, only to end up at Blake's cottage in Sussex, where Mrs. Blake dwells:

> behold me
> Ready to obey, but pity thou my Shadow of Delight:
> Enter my Cottage, comfort her, for she is sick with fatigue.[13]

The two epics differ in presenting the Christian message that unites them and that sets them apart from most of Blake's other works. *Milton* interprets Christianity as self-annihilation and rebirth—as a casting off of the self in a heroic assumption of Eternal Death. But in *Jerusalem*, with its mild, Good-Samaritan Christ who raises the fallen and embraces his bride, the Christianity is not a religion of dying and self-denying heroes but of love and good will, a religion of forgiveness that breaks the chain of revenge and war.

[12] See *Milton*, Plate 38 (Huntington Library copy) and *Jerusalem*, Plates 94, 11, 78. Joseph Wicksteed speculates, brilliantly, that in the Swan-woman Blake bitterly indicts London night-life (*William Blake's Jerusalem* ["The Trianon Press," London, 1955], p. 130). The composite figure, Wicksteed thinks, represents Los (*ibid*, p. 226).
[13] *Milton* II. xxxvi. 30–32, *CW*, p. 527.

The main theme of *Milton* is the restoration of Innocence to life by art.[14] The return to earth of the Poet-Prophet is seen under two aspects: (1) a conquest of the spectral, rational, conventional, neoclassical, natural self by an act of heroic self-denial; (2) a preservation of the natural beauties that supported life in Eden, that bring us intimations of immortality in childhood, that sweeten and hearten an adulthood however repressed, and that will once again flower in the landscape of the New Jerusalem. The first of these is accomplished by the descent of Milton, the second by the descent of the Ololon. The first is sublime, the second beautiful—for Blake, like Fuseli and his generation, was haunted by Burke's distinction, which lies at the base of some of the noblest romantic art.

Milton returns to earth as the artist-Christ—a heroic figure of "terrible majesty."[15] His coming (a sign that the "Last Vintage" approaches)[16] is prepared by Los, the Eternal Prophet, who assumes the role of an Elijah or a John the Baptist in the dying dispensation of Satan. Like all apocalyptic manifestations this one is twofold. On its negative side Milton's coming crushes "the tame high finisher of paltry Blots Indefinite"[17]—proximately Blake's patron Hayley, remotely the entire cultural establishment based on derivative Greco-Roman art and natural religion. On the title page[18] (Plate XXIV) Milton—a purplish nude with the wide almond eye that Blake gave to his Los and to his poet—is about to go to Eternal Death and stands pushing back the clouds of Sinaitic smoke that stands for the moral law and ethical precept.

Milton-Christ descends to die and in dying to destroy Urizen, now a minor figure, and Satan, now a major symbol of corrupt society. Milton is a Mental Traveller, a Pilgrim of Eternity, a Poet, a visionary. Traveling, he creates. Entering space, he makes a womb

---

[14] My concentration on the work of the Prophetic Artist in *Milton* ignores the story of Palamabron and Satan—Blake's version of the Apollo-Phaeton myth that tells how Wrath and Pity became separated. In my judgment Blake has bound this confusing and inconsistent myth to his account of Milton's return only to the detriment of the poem.

[15] *Milton* II. xl. 28, *CW*, p. 532.

[16] *Ibid.*, I. xxiii. 59, *CW*, p. 508.

[17] *Ibid.*, II. xli. 9–10, *CW*, p. 533.

[18] This work of brooding emotion, with its dark ground and white highlights, recalls the chiaroscuro woodcuts of Goltzius (see above pp. 45–47 and Plate XXIX) and also one of Blake's favorite motifs from Raphael's tapestries, the God of Genesis creating the firmament (see above, p. 42 and plate XXII).

and leaves a trail of children. He molds Urizen from the clay of the earth as a sculptor molds his statue, as Jehovah created Adam. But like Los he creates to destroy, and he gives evil a form and substance that can be melted in the fires of the Last Judgment. Thus Milton is both a creating Logos, present in the beginning with the Father, and a dying god, bearing to his own immolation the whole of Satanic society. The very body of Milton contains, grotesquely, the Babylon of sin and law. Milton the creating artist had seen it and had embodied it in his epic and in his life. He now carries it with him to destruction. Like Christ, who bears in his own body on the tree the sins and diseases of the world, so Milton, in the act of destroying his own rational selfishness, destroys the god that had produced it and the society that had nurtured it.

In the other of the two descents described in this poem, the inhabitants of a river in Eden called Ololon follow Milton's example and open a path between earth and heaven, between Great Eternity and the material Polypus. This cloud of sentient life and beauty can enter material reality only by becoming a single twelve-year-old Virgin, who then descends to the roof top of Blake's cottage—and encounters Milton on the strands at Felpham. The host of the Ololon and the Virgin Ololon represent the small life, the natural joys of Blake's world. They are the cumuli of unspoiled nature, the denizens of Leutha where Oothoon met love and was intoxicated by a poetic fancy, the land of the fairies who create books from leaves of flowers. They are the little watchmen of the night, the fireflies; the emmets, the clouds, the lambs; the angels, dragonflies, and splendid-winged butterflies of *Innocence*. They are the "little ones" of *Jerusalem* and *The Four Zoas*, the "minute particulars" of Blake's aesthetics.[19] They symbolize the whole array of life that makes up a sensorium much more vibrant than Sterne's, that whole range of life created by the hammer of Los and sustained by his breath from the tiniest corpuscle of living blood to the great flying eagle—"a portion of Genius; lift up thy head!"[20]

Blake embodies the Innocent life of the Ololon first in the loveliest nature poetry he ever wrote and then in the beautiful washes that diagonally cross the colored page. For these rainbow

[19] See above, pp. 16–18.
[20] *The Marriage of Heaven and Hell* ix. 15, *CW*, p. 152.

hues, more prominent as the climax approaches, do not merely represent the coming apocalyptic dawn but in one of Blake's richest particularities stand for the descent of the Ololon.

Jerusalem fears that her "little ones" may be swallowed up in apocalyptic flame, and Ololon cries out to Milton:

> O where shall I hide my face?
> These tears fall for the little ones, the Children of Jerusalem,
> Lest they be annihilated in thy annihilation.[21]

But though she trembles before the terrible countenance of the hero, she plunges into the "depths of Milton's Shadow, as a Dove upon the stormy Sea."[22] Beauty and sublimity unite, and Los's lark mounts the sky with a loud trill (Plate LXVIII). The question of Blake's most famous lyric has been reversed and answered—he who made the tiger also made the lamb. The new Jerusalem, which saves man from social slavery, will preserve the tender beauties of the old Eden.

Jerusalem, a later, longer, and greater work of prophetic art than *Milton*, tells of Albion's awakening after his sleep of six thousand years, his resurrection from eternal death to eternal life, from Experience to renewed Innocence. The pages—one hundred in all, constituting Blake's longest work of composite art—are of three kinds: the separate illustration with no text, the text with slight but significant borders, and the page with top, middle, or bottom designs. At times the relation between text and design is as close as any Blake ever achieved—as when a verbal metaphor is translated into boldly original lines and rich colors. But often the elements of the form are widely separated—the language of plate eight, for example, is not illustrated until later; or the design strains to express the unvisualizable; or splendors of language are accompanied by unworthy visual motifs.

And yet the gaucheries and irrelevancies are somehow overcome, not so much by the visual brilliance of individual pages as by the cumulative impact of the whole. At the top of a prefatory page (p. 3) in prose, "To the Public," Blake has foreshadowed the Last Judgment by engraving the word *sheep* at the left and the word *goats* at

---

[21] *Milton* II. xl. 14–16, *CW*, p. 532.
[22] *Ibid.*, II. xlii. 5–6, *CW*, p. 534.

the right. These words of division point to one of the most successful artistic qualities of *Jerusalem*, its massing of powerful contrasts—
antithetical visions grandiose in outline and at the same time dense
with vivid details. On one side Blake indicts the present dispensation;
on the other he recalls Eden, anticipates the new Jerusalem, and
celebrates the presence of imaginative vision in the dark night of
man's soul. The first side, which we recognize as Urizenic, Satanic,
and Babylonian, is here called spectral, the spectre being the lower
or rational or selfish side of one's nature—what in biblical terms
would be called the old Adam or the flesh and what Blake sometimes
calls the Selfhood. In contrast to the spectral self is Blake's equivalent of the biblical "spirit," the emanation that arises from both
man and men, the breath and finer spirit of our being and of all
nature, the dreams of the poetic imagination, the intellectual vision
of a purified society.

On the side of spectral goats and demons Blake places such
intellectual movements as classical philosophy and art, Deism, the
thought of Bacon, Locke, Newton, mechanistic science, materialistic psychology, and doubt; such institutions as war, prostitution,
marriage, the human sacrifice of the Druids, the industrial organization of society, the law of Israel; and such psychological states as
the dominance of reason, the tendency to form general intellectual
abstraction and single laws in all humane disciplines, the separation
of wrath and pity, of love and passion. On the side of his emanational
angels and sheep Blake places the imagination, love, forgiveness,
the indestructible individuality of all life however minute, simple
handwork like the hourglass, the child, and the bows and arrows of
intellectual struggle. The spectral side of life is illustrated by rocks,
bat wings, goats, stars, night, nets, black water, snakes, bare trees,
swords, worms, compasses, wheels, oak leaves, beards, crowns,
spiked wheels, caves, dragons, stone temples, scrolls, hoar frost and
mildew, heads without bodies, iron chains, plows, bones, the moon,
staring eyes, Norse gods, and the Venus dei Medici. The emanational side of life is symbolized by Gothic arches, fire, furnaces,
angels, lambs, the sun, grains of sand, the rainbow, light blue—
by many fewer visual symbols, all told, than those that represent
repression. Looking only at the designs, one feels that Blake has
allowed the Urizenic spectres to overwhelm the emanations of Los;
but the words restore the balance, ringing in the new age with the

shout of angel voices. It is most characteristic that the borders and designs embody the suffering present as the words sing the marriage song of the Lamb and of his bride, the New Jerusalem.

Of the innumerable spectral symbols in *Jerusalem*, ranging from tiny bugs that creep in the borders to Druidic serpent temples or cromlechs that dominate whole pages, three are used more continuously and creatively than any of the others. These are *bat wings, vegetable or organic fibers,* and *veils. Bat wings* Blake has elsewhere[23] used with the greatest effect to symbolize institutional tyranny (Plate III). Here the jagged wings, alone or attached to human or animal bodies, dark as night but often embellished with stars and moons, also stand for the debasing power of man's selfish reason and for the debasement of the passions to perverted sexual love (Plate LX). With the *organic fibers* Blake did not achieve the visual success that he did with the wings of bats and evil birds. Sometimes called the stems of vegetation or the weeds of death, they perhaps grow out of one of his oldest symbols of fallen man and nature, the creeper that embraces the tree or the serpent that winds around the human body. In *Jerusalem* Blake's snaky loops have become umbilical cords or intestines that unwind from the human abdomen —grotesque symbols of what binds Albion to the dull diurnal round of a natural life that does not transcend itself or rise to imaginative vision (Plate LVIIIA).

More important than the organic fibers, less successful as visual symbols than the wings, are the *veils* that Blake has made a leitmotif of the language, perhaps the central and controlling symbol of the entire work. This symbol unites with the woman who weaves the veil—one must forgive Blake his pun of *veil* and *Vala*—a mighty goddess who evolved from earthworm to scaled serpent, from serpent to a winged dragon, bright and poisonous, and from dragon to a beautiful and cruel woman, inspired by the scarlet prostitute of the Book of Revelation. Just as Urizen had parodied the patriarch and Satan, the hero, just as the wing of the spectral bat recalls the wing of the eagle who symbolizes genius, so the Babylonian Vala is the false counterpart of the true Jerusalem. She is the "Curtain & Veil & fleshy Tabernacle" that hides the "Divine Vision"[24] in the present dispensation.

[23] See above, pp. 7–8.
[24] *Jerusalem* III. lvi. 40, *CW*, p. 688.

Jerusalem, Albion's emanation who is at once a symbol of lost innocence and of the future paradise, is now a breath, a wraith, an essence.[25] But Vala is all body. She weaves the "nets of beauty & delusion," the moon is her "glimmering Veil," hers is the curtain of shame that Satan placed on Adam and Eve, and her garments must surely recall the "tender curb upon the youthful burning boy" that had made Thel flee in fright from the land of Experience.[26] Vala, one of Blake's richest ambivalences, is an emblem of both frozen chastity and burning prostitution, for it is his meaning that the two inevitably coexist in present society (Plate LVIIIB).

Vala's veils are scarlet and represent official moral virtue that seeks revenge, cruel law, and war. She is the woman in the dragon (an image that seared Blake's imagination), the harlot Babylon, the slayer of Albion's children, the succubus that drinks his blood. She represents man's worst prostitution, the dedication of his skill, his resources, and his fellows to the art of mass destruction.[27]

Although Blake gives to Vala the spindle and distaff of death and so recalls Gray's Fatal Sisters, he does not make her an invincible fate. For Vala's is the veil of the Jewish temple that was rent from top to bottom on the day of the crucifixion.[28] And Blake's final meaning in *Jerusalem* is that just as Urizen was destroyed by Orc, so Vala will be destroyed in mental fight by his spiritual heroes, Christ and Los, never more generously, fully, or powerfully represented than in this his last and greatest prophetic work. Christ appears on the first page of the prophecy proper at the top between a Urizenic star and the crescent moon as a Greek epigraph, Μόνος ὁ Ἰησοῦς ("Jesus only," John 8:9), but he is soon embodied. At the top of one page (p. 31) of stunning contrast he spreads his pierced hands in a gesture of salvation as he swirls downward to the earth, and at the top of another page (p. 33 or 37) he lifts the fallen Albion while at the bottom a hideous batlike spectre hovers over the body of Jerusalem vegetating on the bed of nature in the night of Vala's reign (Plate LIX). In one of Blake's most splendid Crucifixions (p. 76) Christ's body, highlighted in white, hangs on a black cross touched with gold and orange, that resembles both an oak

[25] *Ibid.*, title page, frontispiece, I. xiv. 31–34; IV. lxxxiii. 67, *CW*, pp. 635, 728.

[26] *Ibid.*, IV. lxxix. 78; II. xxxiv. 7; III. lv. 11, *CW*, pp. 721, 660, 686. See *Thel* iv. 19, *CW*, p. 130.

[27] *Jerusalem* I. xxii. 30; I. xxiii. 23; II. xlvii. 12, *CW*, pp. 645, 646, 677.

[28] *Ibid.*, III. lxiv. 32; III. lxvi. 10; II. xxx. 40, *CW*, pp. 699, 702, 656.

tree (representing the Druidic perversion of religion into war) and the huge wings of a spectral bat. Risen Albion emerges from the marbled darkness, looks up, spreads his arms to imitate the cruciform position of the Christ he resembles. Near the end, Christ appears as God the Father, embracing Jerusalem first on a small design of light colors and then in the darkly rich red and yellow flames of the last plate (Plate LXI). Christian love is strong enough to transform Jehovah from the leprous Urizen of Sinai to a forgiving "Universal Father."[29]

In the earlier epic Milton and Christ unite, in the later Los and Christ unite. The meaning is substantially the same in both, that at heart the prophetic and poetic characters are one. In the earlier poem, in which word is more successful than design, it is the poet who unites with Christ; in the later, in which design is, if anything, greater than word, it is the visual artist, the worker in metal, Blake the engraver, that unites with the Divine Humanity. Both poems are tributes to art, for in both the poet-painter is the keeper of the prophet's flame in an age when the dread goddess has extinguished all other lights.

Christ-Jehovah appears on the first and last pages of the prophecy proper, but Los appears on frontispiece and tailpiece and bulks larger in both verse and picture than any other single figure. Without doubt a surrogate for Blake, he suffers division from his emanation, Enitharmon, who is stubborn, jealous, and selfishly independent. He undergoes that curious process of natural enrooting that makes of human form an organic vegetable. In dreadful strife he must conquer the doubts of his own rationalistic spectre, whom he subdues to his own purpose. He must give himself to revolutionary wrath, for he sees that disobedient children can never be reclaimed without authority and that fire must be fought with fire. But for all his agonies and temptations he remains an artist-prophet, loyal to his vision of love and nonviolence, opposing Albion who cries out for an atoning savior. For Los now sees that even atonement is a "Moral Severity" that destroys "Mercy in its Victim."[30]

[29] Ibid., IV. xcvii. 6, CW, p. 744.

[30] Ibid., II. xxxix. 26, CW, p. 666. Later Los refers to the "terrors of Creation & Redemption & Judgment" (IV. xcii. 20, CW, p. 739). Blake once characterized the Atonement as "a horrible Doctrine" (Blake to Crabb Robinson, Arthur Symons, Blake [London, 1907], p. 271).

In the frontispiece (Plate LXIIA) a very human figure, dressed humbly in contemporary dress and wearing the hat of the earthly pilgrim, showing fear on his simple, Cockney face, enters a postern gate. The humble Londoner is really Los. The lantern he carries is a mystical disc (later called a "globe of fire"), the postern gate is Death's Door—its stones suggesting the chains and the spiky wings of Urizenic rule, its shape suggesting the Gothic that will ultimately triumph. In a parallel design (Plate LXIIB) near the end the humble man who had entered the gate with a flickering light emerges as a heroic nude in a blaze of apocalyptic light, bearing a luminous ball, as a Urizenic star and the crescent moon fade on the horizon. Los's *cri du cœur*—"Arise O Lord, & rend the Veil"—has been answered. "Because he kept the Divine Vision in time of trouble," he has been transformed from a humble poetic traveler, not unlike Bunyan's Christian, to a Pilgrim of Eternity. Albion rising from his couch of death to the splendors of unity with himself, his wife, and his children, cries out to Jesus in his final unclouded vision,

I see thee in the likeness & similitude of Los my Friend,

and he wonders equally

at the Divine Mercy & at Los's sublime honour.[31]

[31] *Jerusalem*, II. xxx. 40; IV. xcv. 20; IV. xcvi. 22, 32, *CW*, pp. 656, 742, 743.

CHAPTER IX

Illustrations:
The Book of Job

In a long lifetime devoted to the profession of engraving Blake must have engraved—both from his own and others' designs—some 1,200 illustrations for the work of other writers. Besides these he must have produced well over 500 separate designs and paintings. If one counts all together, one arrives at a figure close to 1,700. Add to this the 375 pages of stereotype engraving that formed his own literary-pictorial canon, and the total mounts to well over 2,000—a figure that dwarfs the mere 38 leaves or so of published unilluminated verse. The lesson of these statistics is clear—Blake's imagination was overwhelmingly committed to visual expression.[1]

Book illustration was the profession that kept Blake alive. Some of it is mere hackwork, like Blake's engraving of Wedgwood's pottery or of antique statues for Rees's *Encyclopedia*. Much else, though competent, remains conventional and uninspired—like Blake's illustrations of the liberal sentimental morality of Mary Wollstonecraft, the supernatural tale of Gottfried Augustus Bürger, the lessons for children of C. G. Salzmann, and the ballads of Hayley. Some illustration is both highly successful and conventional, or at least capable of being interpreted in conventional terms, like the Blair illustrations of 1806, which Fuseli's notes introduce as pious

---

[1] Archibald G. B. Russell, *The Engravings of William Blake* (London, 1912), *passim*; G. E. Bentley, Jr., "Thomas Butts, White Collar Maecenas," *Publications of the Modern Language Association*, LXXI (December, 1956), 1065 and n. 52; W. M. Rossetti, "Annotated Lists of Blake's Paintings, Drawings, and Engravings," in Alexander Gilchrist, *Life of William Blake*, ed. W. Graham Robertson (London and New York, 1907), pp. 415–96 and ed. Ruthven Todd ("Everyman's Library" [London and New York, 1945]), pp. 398–401; Thomas Wright, *The Life of William Blake* (Olney, 1929), II, 128–82. I have omitted from my very approximate but conservative calculations the unpublished verse, illustrated or not—*Vala*, the Rossetti MS, *An Island in the Moon*, the Pickering MS.

sermons, or like the Chaucer painting and engraving of 1810, which Blake himself interprets on principles that would have been fully acceptable to Dr. Johnson and Sir Joshua Reynolds. Sometimes, as in the illustrations to Bunyan and Gay, the work is highly original but unsuccessful: Blake's transcendental radiance awkwardly accompanies the wordly-wise poetry of the Augustan poet. But, though numerous, these and similar works of illustration constitute only a minor portion of a major enterprise that cannot be regarded as merely adjunctive to the true vocation of creating the illuminations. For Blake illustrated Young's *Night Thoughts* with some 537 original watercolors, the Bible with some 200 compositions, Gray in 1800 with 116, Milton from 1808 and on with at least 73, Vergil in 1821 with 17 tiny woodcuts, Job in 1826 with 21 copper cuts, and Dante, a great masterpiece left unfinished at Blake's death, with 102 watercolors, of which only 7 were engraved by Blake and published. Although such monumental works as the designs for Young and Gray were done before Blake had, in *Jerusalem*, closed the canon of his illuminated poetry—thereafter only to produce copies from plates already made—those great masterpieces (illustrations to Milton, Job, Vergil, and Dante) came afterward, suggesting that Blake consciously diverted his creative energies from illumination to illustration.

Whatever his form (wood, copper, or watercolor) and whatever his subject (the uncongenial elegancies of a Gay or the grandest flights of Milton) Blake always displays independence of mind. His style is visible in all his work, even the earliest. Blake's illustrations—either in books or standing alone as separate works of art—illuminate Blake's mind more than the mind of the author he embellishes and should be viewed as elaborations of his mighty myth. Blake produced what his contemporaries called poetical paintings and regarded as the highest form of visual art.[2] Because the visual grammar here is as verbal as the verbal grammar elsewhere is visual, his paintings—as Lamb said of Hogarth's prints—must be read, not viewed. Even the woodcuts illustrating Vergil's

[2] Prince Hoare, who challenged the received opinion that painting must be inspired by poetry and who deplored the universal dogma of the sister arts, conceded that poetical painting is the highest form and that to it the analogy of the arts is relevant (*The Artist; a Collection of Essays, relative to Painting, Poetry, Sculpture, Architecture, the Drama, Discoveries of Sciences, and Various Other Subjects* (London, 1810), I, 1, 14–15, 260–61; II, *passim.*

pastorals—those brooding poems in black and white, so unlike Bewick's—are not untouched by the poet's mind and myth. In one, Blake represents himself walking away from Felpham in a scene (Plate XXXIA) that must be profoundly related to the conclusion of *Milton,* and other of these tiny, simple-seeming designs convey suggestions of prophetic meaning.[3]

Blake's career as a composite artist reached its climax with the illustrations to the Book of Job, his last completed masterpiece. Its several stages, in watercolor first and then copper engraving, occupied the years from approximately 1821 to 1826, years that immediately followed the completion of *Jerusalem.* Decades earlier, in illustrating Edward Young's *Night Thoughts,* Blake had created a private gallery of over five hundred separate rooms—remarkable for their anticipations of the later myth and their transmutation of much poetic lead to visionary gold. The illustrations to Milton's poems, made during the time of the Christian epics, constitute another gallery, not really different in kind from the one created for Young, even though room is tied to room by the harmonious and quiet beauty of the style and by the insistent and recurring suggestion of mythic overtones. It is not until *Job* that Blake, now between the ages of sixty-four and sixty-eight, achieved as an illustrator what he had before only adumbrated—a consecutive visual narrative that possesses symbolic integrity and cumulative artistic force.

BLAKE AND YOUNG

It has been thought that Blake's pictorial giants consort ill with Young's poetic pygmies, to form an ugly and grotesque union. But Young was not a Gay; and his forms, though artistically flaccid, are in imaginative size as large as Blake's. Since Blake owed to Young his conception of Satan as a dunce[4] (Plate LXIII) and some of the most characteristic rhetorical flourishes of his most famous poem, it may be assumed that he approached with sympathy the task of illustrating the poet. The evidence is overwhelming that Blake read Young's verses as the regnant aesthetics dictated they should be read—with a keen eye for their animation and with the ability to translate even their vaguest visual suggestion into full-blown

[3] See above pp. 52–53.
[4] See above, p. 7.

pictorial allegory.[5] Besides, Blake's illustrations, made between 1795 and 1797 when he was at the height of his early prophetic and revolutionary career, constitute a largely unopened gallery, containing many unsurpassed masterpieces and always rich in clues to Blake's symbolism and to the working of his imagination.

In the Young gallery[6] Blake often recalls the schools of art that had formed his mind and style. Medieval architecture is symbolically associated with the hero-poet, and the villainous leering mouth of the classical tragic mask is given to Satan, Charon, and personified Pride. Both the century of the emblem and Blake's own troubled age are present when the artist, in a brilliant revolutionary hieroglyph, translates the words "Lift up your Heads, ye everlasting Gates" into a scene in which a heroic prisoner effectuates his own release as he pulls down a chain that lifts a spiked portcullis resembling the one in the Tower of London. The high Renaissance appears in several female giants that recall Michelangelo's sibyls and in the several adaptations of Raphael's famous tapestry scene that Blake used elsewhere—God separating the light and the dark, the sea and the land (Plates LXIV; cf. Plates XX–XXIV).

The Young illustrations frequently show us the conventional notions from which Blake derived some of his most original and characteristic persons. Young's Brute Matter, Death, "dread Eternity," and Reason produce Blake's Urizen. Discipline becomes a bald Newton with a compass, and Death the Hunter is a youthful beardless Satan wearing a spiked crown. Vala is adumbrated in Pride (a Michelangelesque Delphic priestess), in Reason (a female giant with a scale), in Oppression (a sinister woman with a scaly vest (Plate LXVIA), in Fate (a blonde giantess with a scroll), and in Conscience (a woman clothed with mantle and wings); and Vala is all but created full-blown in the apocalyptic harlot who appears with hideous personifications of the Church, the Law, and the Army (Plate LXV).

The serpent, a clear symbol of brute nature, coils his sinister

[5] See Jean H. Hagstrum, *The Sister Arts* (Chicago, 1958), pp. 266–67.

[6] Most of the 537 original watercolors remain unpublished in the British Museum, Department of Prints and Drawings. But see the engravings that accompanied the edition of Young, printed by R. Noble for Richard Edwards in 1797; Geoffrey Keynes, *Illustrations to Young's Night Thoughts Done in Water-Colour by William Blake* (Cambridge, Mass., 1927); [J. Comyns Carr], "William Blake," *Cornhill Magazine*, XXXI (June, 1875), 721–36.

length in self-defeating circles, and the sunflower stretches out its arms to the Sun. Wit, that quintessentially neoclassic quality, is a cowled man bent in a posture of abject worship before the serpent nature (Plate LXVIB). Blake's Poet—blond, curly, rosy, either nude or in tights—stands for the aspiring mind as he strides across the landscape, a Pilgrim of Eternity, or leaps up from the bondage of matter.

Although Blake respects the poet he illustrates, he sometimes revises and even subverts the meaning of the text. Where Young praises death as a deliverer and a force for good, Blake places Urizen in the landscape. Young says that "*Sense* runs Savage, broke from *Reasons's* chain, / And sings false Peace, till smother'd by the Pall"; but Blake makes Sense a lovely nude who has broken a conventional chain and who is about to be smothered by the huge black and white mantle of Urizen (Plate LXVIIA). Young defends a God in whom Mercy and Justice are blended, satirizing the infidel who makes God all mercy and approving "A God all o'er, consummate, absolute, / Full-Orb'd, in his whole Round of Rays compleat." Blake, the hater of abstraction and stultifying mathematic form, makes Young's God an enormous yellow circle on a tan ground beneath which two figures, slaves of Satan and Urizen, Newton and Locke, crouch in an act of abject worship (Plate LXVIIB).

BLAKE'S MILTON

The Young illustrations were made before Blake went to Felpham—during the period of his revolutionary prophecies. The Milton illustrations—singularly beautiful watercolor designs—are contemporaneous with *Milton* and *Jerusalem*, to whose prophetic message they are surely related. In illustrating the *Nativity Ode* (Plate XI), Blake rejects the classical Apollo and the Druidic religion of the Satanic dragon, and his Christ is both a mild babe born in a Gothic shed and a fiery Orc who leaps out of the furnace of Moloch.[7] Illustrations for *Il Penseroso* (see Plate IV) reflect the moods and themes of Blake's epic, *Milton:* its heroic, sublime side is represented by the poet as Christ in a "rapturous prophetic strain," and the delicate, beautiful Ololon side by the poet surrounded with the spirits of herbs and the flowers. The lark that

[7] *On the Morning of Christ's Nativity: Milton's Hymn with Illustrations by William Blake and a note by Geoffrey Keynes* (Cambridge, 1923), Plates II, V.

rises skyward in the conclusion of the prophecy is surely the *L'Allegro* lark (Plate LXVIII), who as an angel flies against a starry Urizenic sky and startles the dull night (clearly Urizen) from his cloudy watchtower (a version of the Castel Santangelo in Rome, a papal prison, symbolizing religio-political tyranny) as the Poet rises from the ground.[8] The *Comus* illustrations are susceptible of an interpretation that relates them very closely to *Milton* the prophecy. The Attendant Spirit descends to rescue the Lady, as Ololon had descended to rescue Catherine and William Blake from fatigue and discouragement (Plate XXXVII). On the last plate the Lady is restored to her parents in a humble cottage; on the back of a sketch for the last design of *Milton* Blake has written the words, "Father & Mother, I return from flames of fire tried & pure & white." The eight stars of the first *Comus* illustration (where the attendant Spirit flies downward as Comus and his crew revel and the lady sits lost by the root of a tree) may perhaps be the "Eight Immortal Starry-Ones" associated with Ololon and her descent (Plate LXIX).[9]

The illustrations, like the prophecy, grow out of a profound, complex, and lifelong concern with Milton that involved love and hate, inspiration and intellectual struggle. "Milton lov'd me in childhood & shew'd me his face," Blake wrote in 1800,[10] a face that was sometimes that of Los but sometimes that of an old man with a long flowing beard—of Urizen, in fact, for Blake had to confront and reject the Puritan morality of his hero.[11] Philosophical disagreement did not, however, obviate aesthetic harmony. Coming to Milton as a youth belonging to the Wartonian school of literary Miltonism, Blake had always been at ease with the artistic qualities of his master. How comfortably preromantic are Blake's lovely renditions of Milton's personifications—the nunlike Melancholy (a sister of Collins' and Cowper's Evenings) and sprightly Mirth

---

[8] John Milton, *Poems in English with Illustrations by ... Blake* (London, 1926), opp. pp. 28, 38.

[9] C. H. Collins Baker, *Catalogue of William Blake's Drawings and Paintings in the Huntington Library* (San Marino, Calif., 1957), Plates XX–XXVII. See above, pp. 112–13.

[10] Letter to Flaxman, September 12, 1800, *CW*, p. 799.

[11] "I saw Milton in imagination, and he told me to beware of being misled by his Paradise Lost. In particular he wished me to show the falsehood of his doctrine that the pleasures of sex arose from the fall. The fall could not produce any pleasure" (Blake to Crabb Robinson in Arthur Symons, *Blake*, [London, 1907], p. 263).

with her train who belong in the landscape of Gray (Plates IV, XXVIIA).

All of Blake's visual work may be viewed as, in one sense, an illustration of Milton's verbal imagery. Blake's figures "hover on the air, with instruments of music," and his borders recall "the clasping ivy," "the woodbine round the arbour," the "twisted Eglantine," the "two aged Okes," the vine that "curls her tendrils," the "gadding vine" that grows over caves, or the "green mantling vine / That crawls along the side of yon small hill." Blake's serpents also tower "fold above fold, a surging maze," "curl in many a wanton wreath," and wrap themselves around the mossy trunk. Blake's staring tyrants are kings "with awful eye," and his villains, like Milton's Satan, are clothed in "scaly Horrour." Urizenic night is "the starry threshold of Jove's court"; the figures that blast the grain in *Europe* (p. 9) wind, like the gray fly, their sultry horns; and Blake's man lying at the bottom of the sea in *America* (p. 13) recalls Lycidas beneath the watery floor. Milton describes the fig tree whose branching arms are so broad and long,

> that in the ground
> The bended twigs take root, and daughters grow
> About the mother tree, a pillar'd shade
> High over-arch'd . . .[12]

Blake in *The Four Zoas* describes the "root of Mystery accursed shooting up / Branches into the heaven of Los"—branches which,

> pipe form'd, bending down
> Take root again where ever they touch, again branching forth
> In intricate labyrinths o'erspreading many a grizly deep.[13]

The very same passage in Milton that Blake had adapted, Coleridge quoted in the *Biographia Literaria*, calling it "creation rather than painting, or if painting, yet such, and with such co-presence of the whole picture flashed at once upon the eye, as the sun paints in a camera obscura."[14] Milton's verbal picture haunted Blake's painterly fancy, for on the magnificent plate for the twenty-second canto of the *Inferno* ("The Devils with Dante and Vergil, by the

---

[12] *Paradise Lost* ix. 1004–7.
[13] *Vala, or the Four Zoas* vii. 32–35, *CW*, p. 321.
[14] "Everyman's Library" (London, 1906), pp. 238–39.

Side of the Pool") the rock bridges are made to suggest bare trunks that grow in one place, bend over, and take root again in another place to form round arches and spans (Plate LXX). Blake did indeed weave his wild root around the springs of Milton.[15]

The age of Blake was stirred by the interstellar grandeur of Milton's imagination. Fuseli illustrated him with heroic bodies— Michelangelo's prophets performing melodramatic action in violent chiaroscuro—and John Martin created a landscape of enormous, empty, echoing vistas and wastes. But Blake—except for the earlier "House of Death" done in the revolutionary 1790's and except for the terrors expressed in his versions of the encounter of Satan with Sin and Death—laid aside his sublime prophetic manner and brought to *Paradise Lost* lyrical and linear grace, delicacy of watercolor, and ethereal gentleness of body, face, and action. It is as though Blake had determined to soften, humanize, and, by his standards, Christianize his Puritan mentor. Just as he added to his prophetic poem, *Milton*, the beauties and graces of the rainbow-splendid Ololon to mitigate the austerities of his hero's action, so he here accompanies the sublimity of Milton's words with a visual commentary of quiet but profound spirituality. Instead of making of Milton's God an evil Jehovah-Urizen, as he might have done earlier, Blake merely allows the body of Christ to obliterate the face of the deity. The designer's Satan, neither heroic nor fierce, is a young, handsome god in pain and isolation. As Christ routs the rebel angels, Milton's thunders and lightnings are absent, and a mild poet draws a bow of burning gold to shoot an arrow of intellectual desire. God (creating Eve and judging Adam and Eve after the fall) appears as Christ (Plate LXXI). Blake accomplishes the defeat of Urizen and Vala, who lie at the foot of the cross, not by violence but by the self-sacrifice of the Son (Plate LXXII). It would be difficult to find a more benign figure than the military angel Michael, who points to the cross in one scene and leads Adam and Eve out of Eden in another. Even the four Zoas, who appear broodingly in the sky at the time of the expulsion, are not the four horsemen of the Apocalypse, but fallen gods yearning for the day that will restore their primal unity.[16]

[15] See *CW*, p. 414.
[16] Collins Baker, *op. cit.* (n. 9), Plates I–XIII.

It was recorded of Blake shortly after his death that "his greatest pleasure was derived from the Bible—a work ever at hand, and which he often assiduously consulted in several languages."[17] Back of Milton, Michelangelo, and Raphael stood the Hebrew-Christian scriptures, the profoundest single intellectual and moral influence on the man who near the beginning of his career produced a series of Old Testament compositions that attacked the hypocrisy of conventional morality and near its end produced one of his greatest masterpieces of composite art, the *Book of Job*. Between these years Blake created nearly two hundred Bible illustrations in tempera, color-printed drawings, and watercolor.[18] About eighty belong to a series done during and after the Felpham period—watercolor compositions full of the grace and truth of a Fra Angelico that contrast sharply with the temperas (dark, brooding pieces in which the heavy deep colors almost submerge the forms).

As a background for his last work of composite art, Blake's Bible is of interest chiefly for the light it throws on his conception of God the Father, one of the two most important figures in his *Job*. Blake had, for a long and creative period, regarded Jehovah as Urizen, the creator of the material world and the embodiment of legalistic religion. Many of the patriarchs and other Old Testament figures are Urizenic. The white-bearded Abraham of the 1783 watercolor, not fierce but ready to plunge the knife in his son, is proto-Urizenic. Elijah in the chariot of fire, bearded, staring, his hand on a tablet; his *alter ego* Elisha, who receives his blessing; Moses with ropy beard and stony eyes; the stoners of Achan; and the murderer Lamech—all these have been made to resemble the legalistic tyrant of Blake's myth.

But the revolutionary prophetic attack on a tyrannous deity is only one side of Blake's treatment of the Father-God. For though at one extreme there is the haunted and haunting old man forming Adam from the clay of the ground ("Elohim Creating Adam," Plate LXXIII; cf. Plate XLIIB), at the other is "The Angel of the Divine Presence Clothing Adam and Eve," where a benign father, his eyes melting in tenderness, his white beard silky, ministers to the needs of the fallen pair (cf. Plate LXI). David, the early Job,

[17] Symons, *op. cit.* (n. 11), p. 373.
[18] Geoffrey Keynes, *William Blake's Illustrations to the Bible* (London, 1957).

the haloed and grieving Ezekiel seem to be men of dignity and goodness; the father in white in Innocence rescues the erring and appears in the chimney sweeper's dream. It could not have been otherwise for anyone trained in the Christian tradition. The father-figure would inevitably be associated with tenderness and love even at the very moment it was used as the symbol of a perverting society.

The paradox, a profound one that Blake could not let stand unresolved, occupies the very center of his myth where there are two fathers. One, who is created by Satan-Urizen and by man's spectral reason, wrote the law of prohibition and revenge. The other, created by the artist-Christ and by man's visionary imagination, repented of writing the law, hid it beneath the mercy seat, and established the covenant of forgiveness. Man's salvation lies in choosing which of these deities to worship—the leprous pestilential Jehovah of the Lazar House or the Jehovah who embraces the fallen Jerusalem and restores Eden (Plates XLIIB, LXI). Blake's myth says that both man and his God need to be redeemed. The salvation of one implies the salvation of the other. Man creates God in his image, but that God also creates man in his—for, as Blake says repeatedly, we become what we behold.

The transformation of Jehovah from a Urizenic tyrant to a God of forgiveness and of his worshiper from a Urizenic victim to a proud and artistically productive "Christian" is the theme of Blake's *Job*. It tells of the casting out of the spirit of "evil in things heavenly," to use the words of *Ephesians* that appeared on the title page of *The Four Zoas;* or, in Blake's own terminology, the casting out by man of his selfish, conventional, unimaginative, and rationalistic self, as Los subdued his spectre by the furnaces in *Jerusalem*. That spectre, who says of himself, "I am Despair," says of God:

> For he is Righteous, he is not a Being of Pity & Compassion,
> He cannot feel Distress, he feeds on Sacrifice & Offering,
> Delighting in cries & tears & clothed in holiness and solitude.[19]

But Los, the force of whose hammer is eternal forgiveness, throws out his spectre and all it stands for, and finally says,

> there is no other
> God than that God who is the intellectual fountain of Humanity.[20]

[19] *Jerusalem* I. x. 47–49, *CW*, p. 630.
[20] *Ibid.*, IV. lxxxviii. 50; IV. xci. 10–11, *CW*, pp. 734, 738.

Blake's *Job* records the substitution of Los's God for that of his spectre.

Job is a work of composite art that consists of several minor characters, two major ones, and an allegorical landscape. Among the minor characters, the most important is Satan, who appears first as a young man of heroic shape but who soon becomes a grinning demon, the enemy of joy, the leprous spreader of plague, and a scaly military creature, who is expelled in flames. Socially, he is the personification of evil society. Ontologically, he stands for evil, only superficially for the natural evil of plague and catastrophe, more profoundly for the evil that persuades man to persecute and torture himself and to make his life a bed of pain and a hell of repressed desire.

The emblematic, unpicturesque landscape powerfully enforces Blake's meaning. In the opening scene the sun sets (left) over a Gothic church, and a Urizenic moon and star rise (Plate LXXIV). In the last scene, with positions reversed, the star and moon set and the sun of redemption rises on a new day (Plate LXXX). While Satan directs man's will against himself, a Urizenic-Satanic landscape predominates—heavy Druidic stones dwarf the good Gothic church; barren rocks, cromlechs, ruined buildings, stormy or starry skies replace the kindly animals and the spreading vegetation of *Innocence*.

God is an exact image of Job. So close is the resemblance between the two that only iconic accompaniments and position in the design make them distinguishable. Blake, a sketchy delineator of emotion in the face, does not always make his precise intentions clear; but the God who acquiesces in the torture of Job is indisputably Urizenic. As he haunts Job in dreadful dreams he recalls the Elohim that created Adam. God finally, however, assumes the benignity we had felt him to possess all along, and in our last view of him he has become Christlike. The universe has been purged of cruel holiness and crippling convention.

God is as Job perceives him to be, and it is Job who is the hero of the story. He begins as a victim of Urizenic religion—old, bearded, holding an open book before him. His eyes are raised in the pious expression neoclassical culture admired in the Christs and saints of Guido Reni and other eclectic masters of Bologna. As Job's adversities multiply, he responds as any abject Urizenic worshiper would. He prays, gives charity, weeps, lifts his hands in despair, accepts the taunts of his friends, and continues to look, in feeble piety, to the heaven that has betrayed him. Our sympathy for him quickens when God tortures him and when, sitting in upright dignity and bearing the marks of suffering in his eyes, he shows that the Urizenic religion that has tortured his body and repressed his joys has not subdued his mind. Now a humble man but not an abject one, he receives charity and rises through successive stages to the dignity of artistic religion in a purely human and natural society where God exists only in the imaginative life of man.

Job is a highly original work of integrated art. The relation between words, borders, scenes, and abstract designs is radically different from the form of the earlier illuminations. The illuminations began as poems to which scene and border were added. *Job* began as a series of watercolor paintings and became composite art only as text and border were added in the engraved state.[21] The earlier illuminations were made in stereotype relief, produced by an acid bath, with color usually added to the final version. *Job* is a work of black and white line engraving on copper, the intaglios cut out of the metal by the burin only. In the illuminations the verbal text stands at the center and carries the narrative. The border motifs and figures that surround the centrally placed poem may impinge upon it, divide it into stanzas, and interpret it; but they never challenge the centrality of the word. That relation has been reversed in *Job*, where the design is central and carries the narrative, while the words appear in the border and have the suggestive quality of design. For they are brief, proverbial, and gnomic, and come from various places in the Bible to universalize the meaning. The new form reminds one of the relation of word and design in the emblem, the *impresa*, and the moral narratives of Hogarth, where words appear as *mots*, posies, or versicles and are usually subordinate to the picture or design.

Blake had earlier experimented with coherent visual narrative. The Young illustrations illuminate only the single line, couplet, or phrase which Blake usually marked with an asterisk; and, though

---

[21] *Illustrations of the Book of Job by William Blake; Being All the Water-Colour Designs Pencil Drawings and Engravings Reproduced in Facsimile with an Introduction by Laurence Binyon . . . and Geoffrey Keynes* ("The Pierpont Morgan Library" [New York 1935]).

motifs are repeated from design to design, the compositions form no narrative or logical sequence. But in the emblem series, "The Gates of Paradise" (1793), cryptic allegory is obscurely but consecutively revealed.[22] The Blair illustrations were presented to the public as, quite apart from the verse of the *Grave*, constituting "of themselves a most interesting Poem."[23] None of these anticipates the visual narrative of *Job* so clearly as do Blake's illustrations of the "Ode on the Death of a Favourite Cat, Drowned in a Tub of Gold Fishes."[24] Gray's witty narrative, embellished with neoclassical artificiality, is a warning to the fair to beware of one false step and to remember that all that glisters is not gold. Blake transforms this neoclassical *jeu d'esprit* to a grimly ironic story of the fall of one of Albion's daughters, told in a series of narrative designs. (1) A tabby cat with incipient wings, wearing a bonnet and shawl, looks into the water in which swim two of Blake's sinister Urizenic creatures with goggle-eyes and batlike fins. (2) A nude woman, replacing the cat who had suggested a woman, now sits squarely on the back of the cat, while below swim two fish with women on their backs. (3) The cat is now a woman alone who reclines on the edge of a pool and regards her image in the water while under a lake flower a winged boy and girl embrace. (4) The cat now reappears accompanied by a woman representing Fate while in the water below swim two attractive children with huge bat wings. (5) Fate now pushes the woman, a cat no longer, headlong into the water, and the two figures rise as military tyrants, bearing spear and shield. (6) The fish are now for the first time fish and nothing else, as the maiden folds her hands in prayer and lifts her head heavenward, and the curtain falls on a brief narrative of how society represses love.

Blake's visual fable stands to Gray's *vers de société* as Blake's *Job* stands to its biblical original. The Bible provides only the sketchiest narrative outline and the characters; Blake provides new meanings in a new form.[25]

[22] Geoffrey Keynes (ed.), *William Blake's Engravings* (London, 1950), Plates 8–28.
[23] Robert Blair, *The Grave: A Poem, Illustrated by Twelve Etchings* (London, 1808), p. 33.
[24] H. J. C. Grierson (ed.), *William Blake's Designs for Gray's Poems* (Oxford, 1922).
[25] See Joseph H. Wicksteed's pioneer study, *Blake's Vision of the Book of Job* (London and New York, 1910).

On the title page, the only plate in this series in which word is central and design peripheral, flamelike Hebrew letters and English letters in Gothic style symbolize two of Blake's staunchest symbols of the good life of vision. (The Hebrew scriptures and medieval art are always opposed to naturalistic or classical culture, which is incapable of perceiving such realities behind and within nature as angels with flame-tipped, Gothic-shaped wings who form a circle of descent and ascent around the words.) On page one (1) Job and his family appear as a pious, not a happy family (Plate LXXIV). Musical instruments hang unused on the tree—which with its prominent branches may stand for institutional religion—and Urizenic books are open on the parents' knees, for it is a culture in which the "letter killeth." Wife and sons kneel and pray, while sheep drowse and Job looks upward in conventional piety. The very slight border reminds us, in its upward-sweeping triangle, of the tents of Israel, here surely the tents of prosperity and divine favor, for the fire of sacrifice burns between two sacrificial animals and Job has many sheep. (2) Job continues to live in bookish piety and material wealth, while before God, who also bears an open book on his lap, Satan appears in flame, accompanied by the faces of Urizen and the Harlot of Babylon, all three symbols of the prostituted or "chartered" society. In contrast, the border designs are pastoral and imply Gothic design and Hebrew vision, though the Hebrew letters at the top—"Jehovah is King"—remind us that the society is conventionally Urizenic and pious. Scroll-bearing angels, whose wings faintly suggest Sinaitic tablets, have just touched the earth in front of Job. (3) Satan, handsome and young in his first appearance, is now sooty and bat-winged (Plate LXXV), spreading with his hands the fires of misery. He is a societal Satan who wreaks angry and destructive judgment on music, sexual pleasure, and joy, and who is only partially frustrated by one of Job's sons, a poetic-heroic type suggesting Los, who ministers to the suffering children of Job-Albion. (4) Satan, now bearing a military sword and wearing bat-wings, is moved to the borders, while in the main design a messenger, Blake's poet-traveler—with Gothic spires and a running boy (auguries of Innocence in the Urizenic desert) as background—reports disasters to Job and his wife, more obviously pious than ever as they lift their eyes and hands heavenward while seated under a bare tree of Experience and on a stony Druidic seat. (5) Job's divinely permitted and Satanically induced sufferings have reduced him to that state of Urizenic humility that will

> Boast of high Things with Humble tone,
> And give with Charity a Stone,[26]

charity received by a Urizenic victim (like the old man who stands for London in both *Experience* and *Jerusalem*) while conventional angels look on, while a dismayed and helpless God almost slips from his throne, and while Satan is about to pour his vials in Job's ear. (6) Satan, his body scaly (Plate LXXVI), releases his pestilences upon Job, who is more anguished than ever but also more pious than ever ("Blessed be the name of the Lord," says a border text) as his wife adopts the posture of a Urizenic sufferer, as the landscape becomes bleaker and stonier, and as border angels with Newtonian bat-wings drop spider-like plummets to the earth below. (7) Grieving angels replace Newtonian angels in the top corners and an old and a young shepherd mourn in the bottom corners while Job's friends —"Corporeal Friends are Spiritual Enemies"—appear before the sufferer with angry patriarchal faces and pious hands raised skyward. (8) It is Job's turn to weep and raise his hands, as he curses his birthday. Wife and friends kneel in Urizenic grief in a stony, dark, and forbidding landscape, that border texts and motifs— mushrooms, cactus, and toadstool—do nothing to relieve. (9) As Eliphaz rebukes Job and invokes a stern vision of a God that resembles him in moral severity, Job and his wife look quizzically skyward to see nothing but repressive old men (Plate LXXVII). (10) In contrast to the Three Accusers of Sin (according to Blake, legalistic creators of sin) Job appears a sympathetic figure with merciful eyes and a wounded but persisting dignity. (11) Having seen Eliphaz' God of unrelenting justice and having been accused of sin by his patriarchal councillors, Blake now has his own vision— and a frightening one it is (Plate LXXVIII; cf. Plates XLIIB, LXV, LXVIIA). God, with cloven hoof and flaming hair, appears wrapped in a serpent of natural religion and points to the tablets of religious law as he threatens his victim with the hell that Job sees from his couch; from hell's lake of flame demons rise with chains

---

[26] "The Everlasting Gospel" (version *d*), ll. 3–4, *CW*, p. 751.

and scaly arms to pull Job down.[27] This is the climax of Job's
sufferings—to be tormented and threatened by a cruel god whom
he still resembles. (12) In refreshing contrast Job is now approached
by Elihu, Blake's poet-type, who in starry Urizenic darkness
silences the councillors and points upward; tiny angels rise in the
border from a Urizenic figure sleeping at the bottom, to form a
pointed Gothic arch. The border texts here give assurance of a
gentler deity than the one we have seen. (13) The God that answers
Job out of the whirlwind is not the God that tortured him upon his
bed with visions of hell, but a man with merciful eyes, who is close
to earth, his arms outstretched in recollection of Christ's position on
the cross (cf. Plate LXXII). The God of the design anticipates the
new, but the God of the border is the old Urizen swirling about,
in nature's eternal round, a classic and Druidic arch. (14) Job and
his friends remain in a cloudy earth-cave, but God now commissions
Apollo and Diana, the sun and the moon, Los and Enitharmon, while
the morning stars in the form of Gothic angels sing together at the
top. (15) As bearded angels write in their Urizenic books, God now
shows Job and his friends the circle of nature below them, not, as
in the Bible, to overawe human weakness and teach sublime
resignation, but to show that there is no hope in material nature as it
is—a round ball filled with two monsters of warlike power, a
Babylonish realm of war by land (the Behemoth) and war by sea (the
Leviathan).[28] (16) As Job and his wife observe the scene with serene
wonder and as the friends twist their bodies in terror, Satan and his
minions are cast into the flames—an action in which God purifies
the world by purifying himself and casting out Satanic error. Blake's
Last Judgment does not punish the wicked but it dethrones error
as good art overcomes bad art (cf. Plate XI). (17) A purified vision
of God (cf. Plate LXXI) as Christ now blesses Job and his wife and
frightens the worldly councillors, while in the bottom border books
with the Johannine gospel of love have replaced the books of stony
law. (18) Having appeared as Christ, God disappears now from the
plates in separate anthropomorphic form. In Job's sacrifice the

[27] Cf. letter to Flaxman, September 12, 1800: "terrors appear'd in the Heavens
above / And in Hell beneath," *CW*, p. 799.

[28] In *Jerusalem* Los's rationalistic spectre forms "Leviathan / And Behemoth, the
War by Sea enormous & the War / By Land astounding" (IV. xci. 39–41, *CW*,
p. 738).

pyramidal flame rises from a stone altar to an abstract radiance. Artist's pallet and the open book of the gospel lie in the bottom border. (19) The man who in the Urizenic dispensation gave false charity now receives true charity with dignity, as the forms at the bottom, recalling the Earth of *Experience*, now awake and scatter abundance, and as angels rise from palm-tree borders to form an authentic Gothic design. (20) Job, his daughters at his side, now lifts his arms as God had done in the whirlwind and points to wall scenes that represent his past—the day of his suffering, the day of God's appearance, and, finally, in a scene recalling Blake's famous representation of himself being inspired by Milton,[29] a poet receiving the inspiration of Los (Plate LXXIX). Like Los defeating evil by giving it form Job the artist has transcended his experiences by shaping them, and Urizen is now imprisoned in a wall design near the floor. (21) The casting out of evil by art having been portrayed by the artist-Job on the walls of his house, he now joins his family in the Christian life of music and song (Plate LXXX). The sun that was setting in the first plate now rises, and the Urizenic star and moon which rose in the first now set. The instruments that hung useless on the tree of institutional religion now are used by the happy united family, and the burnt offerings, which appeared in the same position on the first plate, are now negated by the accompanying text, "In burnt Offerings for Sin Thou hast had no Pleasure." Institutional ritual that had made the family kneel in prayer has been replaced by uninhibited artistic expression in which Job, his wife, and his children stand to sing and play.

As Blake said, the only true Christian is the artist, and the only true God, the God in man. *Job* began with a two-dimensional universe in which man knelt in prayer; it ends without a material manifestation of God; now man stands to create art. Christ, though absent, remains in the effect. Blake once called him "the only God," but added quickly, "And so am I and so are you."[30]

[29] *Milton*, Plate 29 (Huntington Library copy).
[30] Blake to Crabb Robinson in Symons, *op. cit.* (n. 11), p. 255. "I know of no other Christianity ... than the liberty ... to exercise the Divine Arts of Imagination." Cf. *Jerusalem* IV. lxxvii, *CW*, pp. 716–17.

Conclusion

Sir,

    I send you a List of the different Works you have done me the honour to enquire after. . . . Those I printed for Mr Humphry are a selection from the different Books of such as could be Printed without the Writing, tho' to the Loss of some of the best things. For they when Printed perfect accompany Poetical Personifications & Acts, without which Poems they never could have been Executed.

Blake to Dawson Turner, June 9, 1818

CHAPTER X

Poet-Painter

Why does Blake score his page with lines and stain it with color?

His profession was to engrave illustrations for printed books, and as an engraver he was intimately familiar with emblems, devices, borders, and a thousand embellishments that could adorn and interpret the printed page. As a friend of the Edwardses and perhaps of Gough, as an apprentice of Basire and a student of Pars, he was early intimate with classical and medieval remains, and may have seen the original splendors of medieval illumination. Blake viewed his poetic hero, John Milton, in the personifying, pictorialist vision of the preromantics; and it took no great imaginative leap to link the author of *Paradise Lost* with the greatest masters of his pictorial pantheon—the Dürer who engraved sacred story, the Raphael whose tapestries were transformed into a pictorial Bible, the Michelangelo who put his version of Genesis and Revelation on the Sistine walls and ceiling. The friend of Fuseli and Barry could hardly have done other than to *see* sacred story and to present the truth he had come to know by ear and eye in both verbal and visual language.

Blake wanted his message to attack the whole man—all at once. He must have thought it served his purpose as a prophet to invade man's soul by the avenues of more than one sense, and he makes his psychological assault frontal, the better to accomplish his purpose. If under Urizen man's senses have been starved, the art that fed more than one was likelier than poetry alone to bring nourishment to the soul and to arouse the dormant faculties. Blake's art, like his thought, moves towards fusion—but a fusion that never destroys particularity and identity. Verbal art alone can become abstract in a way that verbal-visual art cannot—particularly an art that never deserts natural forms for mystical abstractions and signs.

It was Blake's mission to preserve and refine Innocence—to carry it intact and fresh through the death-valley of Experience into

the new Eden, where it becomes imperishable. The very breath
and finer spirit of both the new and the old Innocence is Imagination,
and Experience cannot be more succinctly described than to call it
the death of the artistic spirit. God is man, and the true man is the
Poetic Genius. Blake is Los and Los is Christ, and the Everlasting
Gospel is the practice of the imagination. The Last Judgment is
the casting out of bad art by good, and the New Jerusalem rewards
the prophet who has kept faith with vision in the time of great
tribulation.

To achieve these high ends of Mental Fight, Blake's composite
art served as the chief weapon. The tiny stereotypes of 1788
attacked in line and word the established materialistic psychology
as a stifler of imaginative vision. The luminous pages of the Stirling
Jerusalem dissolved the old in apocalyptic fire; and in its own color,
line, and song provided an earnest of the glorious liberty of the sons
of Los. The sword that Blake would not allow to sleep in his hand
was two-edged, and the Chariot of Fire was drawn by two horses.
For Blake was more than a poet who happened also to be a painter.
He molded the sister arts, as they have never been before or since,
into a single body and breathed into it the breath of life.

Blake wrote once about two smiles that formed one smile—a
Smile of Smiles. Blake's union of the arts created a new form—an
Art of Arts that also

> . . . sticks in the Heart's deep Core
> And it sticks in the deep Back bone.[1]

[1] "The Smile," ll. 9–10, *CW*, p. 423.

Illustrations

I Blake, *The Book of Urizen*

To The Accuser who is
The God of This World

Truly My Satan. thou art but a Dunce
And dost not know the Garment from the Man
Every Harlot was a Virgin once
Nor canst thou ever change Kate into Nan

Tho thou art Worshipd by the Names Divine
Of Jesus & Jehovah: thou art still
The Son of Morn in weary Nights decline
The lost Travellers Dream under the Hill

II Blake, *For the Sexes: The Gates of Paradise*

III   Blake, *Europe*

IV   Blake, *Il Penseroso*

V A   Blake, *For the Sexes: The Gates of Paradise*

V B   Blake, *There Is No Natural Religion*

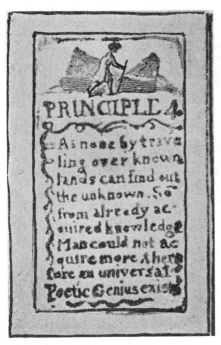

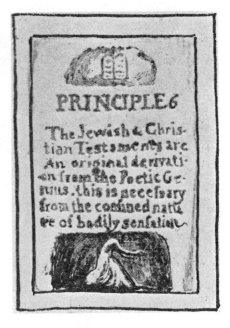

V C   Blake, *All Religions Are One*

V D   Blake, *All Religions Are One*

VI   Blake, *The Song of Los*

ASIA

The Kings of Asia heard
The howl rise up from Europe!
And each ran out from his Web;
From his ancient woven Den;
For the darkness of Asia was startled
At the thick-flaming, thought-creating fires of Orc.

And the Kings of Asia stood
And cried in bitterness of soul.

Shall not the King call for Famine from the heath?
Nor the Priest, for Pestilence from the fen?
To restrain! to dismay! to thin!
The inhabitants of mountain and plain;
In the day of full-feeding prosperity;
And the night of delicious songs.

Shall not the Councellor throw his curb
Of Poverty on the laborious?
To fix the price of labour;
To invent allegoric riches:

And the privy admonishers of men
Call for Fires in the City
For heaps of smoking ruins,
In the night of prosperity & wantonness.

To turn man from his path,
To restrain the child from the womb,

VII   Blake, *The Song of Los*

UT PICTURA POESIS ERIT.

Horace

IX *Collection of Etruscan, Greek, and Roman Antiquities*

X   Stuart and Revett, *Antiquities of Athens*

XI Blake, *Nativity Ode*

XII   The Bedford Hours

XIII   The Bedford Hours

XIV A   The Bedford Hours

XIV B   The Bedford Hours

XIV c   The Bedford Hours

XIV d   The Bedford Hours

XV   Blake, "The River of Life"

XVI Dürer, "The Penance of St. John Chrysostom"

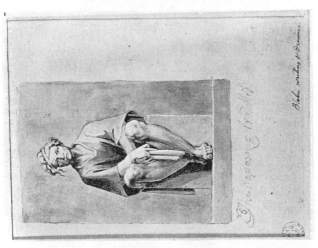

XVII c   Fuseli, *Pericles*

XVII b   Blake after Michelangelo, "The Reposing Traveller"

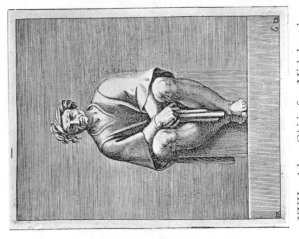

XVII a Adam Ghisi after Michelangelo

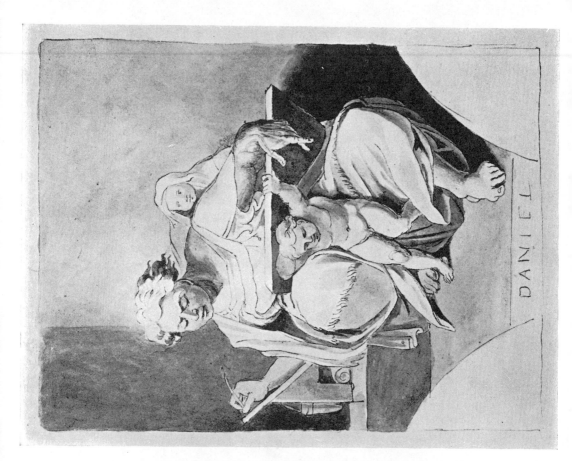

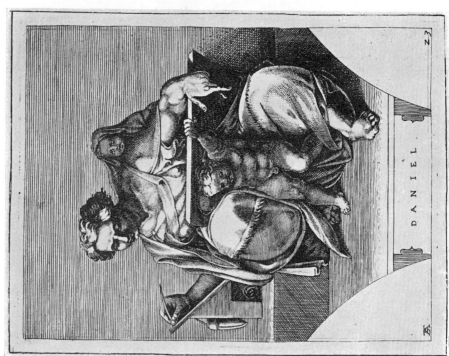

XIX B   Marco da Ravenna after Raphael

XIX A   Marcantonio Raimondi after Raphael

XX   De Rubeis after Raphael, *Imagines Veteris ac Novi Testamenti*

XXI Blake, *The Book of Urizen*

XXII   De Rubeis after Raphael, *Imagines Veteris ac Novi Testamenti*

Urizen C: V.

The Nostrils bent down to the deep. In trembling; & howling & dismay.
And a fifth Age passed over; And a seventh Age passed over:
And a state of dismal woe. And a state of dismal woe.

11. In ghastly torment sick; Chap: V.
Within his ribs bloated round.
A craving Hungry Cavern. 1. In terrors Los shrunk from his
Thence arose his channeld Throat. task:
And like a red flame a Tongue His great hammer fell from his hand:
Of thirst & of hunger appeard. His fires beheld, and sickening,
And a sixth Age passed over: Hid their strong limbs in smoke.
And a state of dismal woe. For with noises ruinous loud;
 With hurtlings & clashings & groans
12. Enraged & stifled with torment The Immortal endur'd his chains,
He threw his right Arm to the north Tho' bound in a deadly sleep.
His left Arm to the south
Shooting out in anguish deep. 2. All the myriads of Eternity,
And his Feet stampd the nether Abyss All the wisdom & joy of life;
 Roll like a sea around him.

Except what his little orbs Then he lookd back with anxious desire
Of sight by degrees unfold. But the space undivided by existence
 Struck horror into his soul.
3. And now his eternal life
Like a dream was obliterated 6. Los wept obscur'd with mourning;
 His bosom earthquakd with sighs
4. Shuddring, the Eternal Prophet smote He saw Urizen deadly black,
With a stroke, from his north to south In his chains bound, & Pity began.
 region
The bellows & hammer are silent now In anguish dividing & dividing
A paralels silence, his prophetic voice For pity divides the soul
Siezd; a cold solitude & dark void In pangs eternity on eternity
The Eternal Prophet & Urizen closd Life in cataracts pourd down his
 cliffs
5. Ages on ages rolld over them The void shrunk the lymph into Nerves
Cut off from life & light frozen Wandring wide on the bosom of night
Into horrible forms of deformity And left a round globe of blood
Los sufferd his fires to decay Trembling upon the Void

XXIII   Blake, *The Book of Urizen*

XXIV Blake, *Milton*

XXV   Giorgio Ghisi after Giulio Romano

Cohors Cetrata, breuibus scutis lunatis, quæ Cetræ, seu Peltæ vocabant, armata.
Alia Cohors cum scutis oblongis octogonis Germanorum veterum. Iide loricas hamatas habent, quas circuli, siue anuli ferrei, instar squammarum nectunt.

XXVI   Petro Bartolo after Giulio Romano

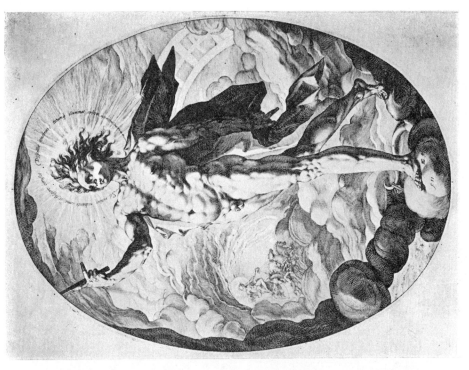

XXVII b Goltzius, "The Sun God"

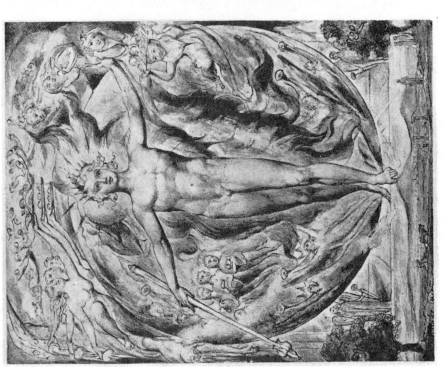

XXVII a Blake, *L'Allegro*

XXVIII B Blake, *The Book of Urizen*

XXVIII A Goltzius, "Tantalus"

XXIX   Goltzius, "The Magician"

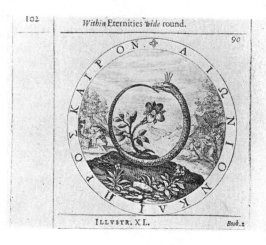

left XXX A   Quarles, *Emblemes*

right XXX B   Wither, *A Collection of Embleme*

bottom XXX C   Cats, *Silenus Alcibiadis*

XXXI A   Blake, *Vergil*   XXXI B   Blake, *Vergil*

XXXII   John Speed, Map of Denmark

XXXIII   Blake, *Jerusalem*

XXXIV   Blake, *Songs of Innocence*

They laugh at our play,
And soon they all say,
Such such were the joys.
When we all girls & boys.
In our youth time were seen,
On the Ecchoing Green.

Till the little ones weary
No more can be merry
The sun does descend,
And our sports have an end:
Round the laps of their mothers.
Many sisters and brothers,
Like birds in their nest.
Are ready for rest:
And sport no more seen,
On the darkening Green.

XXXV   Blake, *Songs of Innocence*

Subsequent printers (especially Godard*) enlarged these astrological figures, adopting however the same expression of character.

Let me now direct your attention to decorations of a more pleasing description. First, then, we will fancy ourselves strolling in some

'garden tempting with forbidden fruit,'

and witnessing the agility with which yonder youths are climbing the tree, and stealing the said 'forbidden fruit.' Observe also the cunning and cautious manner in which a fair *damoiselle* catches the falling treasures in her lap! Few embellishments were more popular, for a series of years;† and renowned WILLIAM LILY has taken care that future generations should be made acquainted with so tempting an illustration. What you here see, is taken from a Missal, printed by Verard, of the date of 1498.

* See page 88, ante.

† *Few embellishments were more popular, for a series of years;*] In fact, the above embellishment, modified and enlarged, formed the title-page to the celebrated LILY'S GRAMMAR; and is even yet 'made familiar to youth.' A distinguished modern writer has contrived, with some felicity, to illustrate this apple-stealing frontispiece. Describing the march of the allies to Paris, after the ever-memorable battle of Waterloo, he observes that it was 'no great degradation from the discipline of the English army to remark, that some old school-boy practices were not forgotten; and that, where there occurred a halt, and fruit-trees happened to be in the vicinity, they instantly were loaded like the epigrammatic tree in *Lily's Grammar*, only with soldiers instead of scholars; and surrounded by their wives, who held their aprons to receive the fruit instead of satchels, as in the emblem chosen by the learned grammarian.' *Paul's Letters to his Kinsfolk,*

left XXXVI A William Lily, *A Short Introduction of Grammar*

right XXXVI B Dibdin *Bibliographical Decameron*

Ecce Puer, fructus, ad quos hulî ipse Magister,
Et Pater invitant, & bene notus Amor.

Sæpe ulta est raptos crudelis Betula malos,
Nunc ut damites verbera, carpe Puer.
TW

XXXVII Blake, *Comus*

Salvator Rosa delin: Neagle sculp.

Engraved for MAYNARD's Josephus.

The APPARITION of SAMUEL raised by the WITCH of ENDOR
at the request of King Saul.

XXXVIIIB   Maynard and Kimpton, *Works of Josephus*

Metz delin: Blake sculp.

Engraved for MAYNARD's Josephus.

THE FUGITIVE SHECHEMITES
Buried and suffocated in the Holds of their Retreat
by order of King Abimelech.

XXXVIIIA   Maynard and Kimpton, *Works of Josephus*

XXXIX   Woollett after Hannan, "Gardens of Sir Francis Dashwood"

XL b   Barry, "Job Reproved by his Friends"

XL a   Barry, "Neptune"

A Dropping room

—Jelly ever has a wanton stare
A wispering wantoness and a trifling air
But nummour whilst amove cost
Untighten by engaging our repost

XLI b   Rhodes after Fuseli,
Poems by Cowper

XLI a   Mortimer, "Nebuchadnezzar"

XLII A   Fuseli or Blake, "The House of Death"

XLII B   Blake, "The House of Death"

Infant Joy

I have no name.
I am but two days old.—
What shall I call thee?
I happy am
Joy is my name,—
Sweet joy befall thee!

Pretty joy!
Sweet joy but two days old,
Sweet joy I call thee:
Thou dost smile.
I sing the while
Sweet joy befall thee.

XLIII   Blake, *Songs of Innocence*

The Divine Image.

To Mercy Pity Peace and Love,
All pray in their distress:
And to these virtues of delight
Return their thankfulness.

For Mercy Pity Peace and Love,
Is God our father dear:
And Mercy Pity Peace and Love,
Is Man his child and care.

For Mercy has a human heart
Pity, a human face:
And Love, the human form divine,
And Peace, the human dress.

Then every man of every clime,
That prays in his distress,
Prays to the human form divine
Love Mercy Pity Peace.

And all must love the human form,
In heathen, turk or jew
Where Mercy, Love & Pity dwell,
There God is dwelling too.

XLIV   Blake, *Songs of Innocence*

The Blossom.

Merry Merry Sparrow
Under leaves so green
A happy Blossom
Sees you swift as arrow
Seek your cradle narrow
Near my Bosom.

Pretty Pretty Robin
Under leaves so green
A happy Blossom
Hears you sobbing sobbing
Pretty Pretty Robin
Near my Bosom.

XLV   Blake, *Songs of Innocence*

XLVI Blake, *Songs of Innocence and Experience*

The SICK ROSE

O Rose thou art sick.
The invisible worm.
That flies in the night
In the howling storm:

Has found out thy bed
Of crimson joy:
And his dark secret love
Does thy life destroy.

XLVII   Blake, *Songs of Innocence and Experience*

The Author & Printer Willm Blake. 1789.

2

XLVIII   Blake, *The Book of Thel*

XLIX A *Le Antichità di Ercolano Esposte*

XLIX B Blake, *The Book of Thel*

L   Blake, *The Marriage of Heaven and Hell*

LII   Blake, *Visions of the Daughters of Albion*

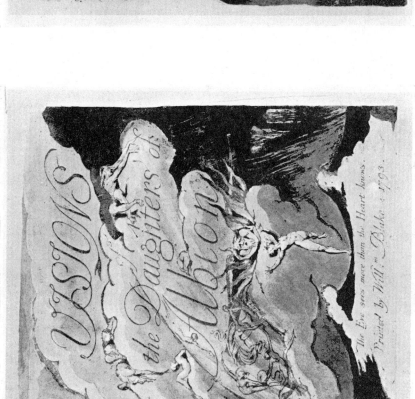

LIII b   Blake, *Visions of the Daughters of Albion*

LIII a   Blake, *Visions of the Daughters of Albion*

LV a   Blake, *America*

LV b   Blake, *America*

TAB.V. *p .52.*

An antient Altar in Alabaster Dedicated to
St John Bapt: in poßeßion of W. Stukeley.
Inscribed to the learned Samuel Gale Esqr

LVI   William Stukeley, *Palaeographia Britannica*

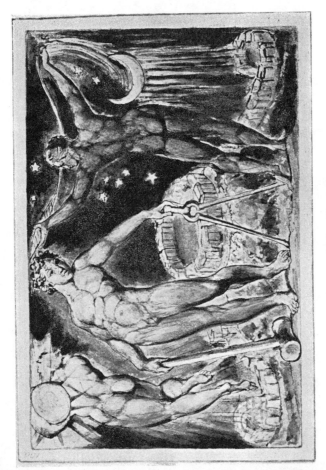

LVII B Blake, *Jerusalem*

LVII A Blake, *The Book of Urizen*

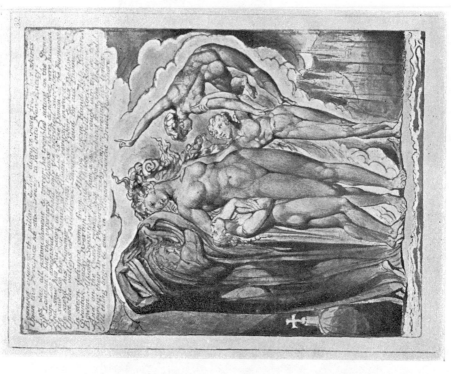

LVIII B　Blake, *Jerusalem*

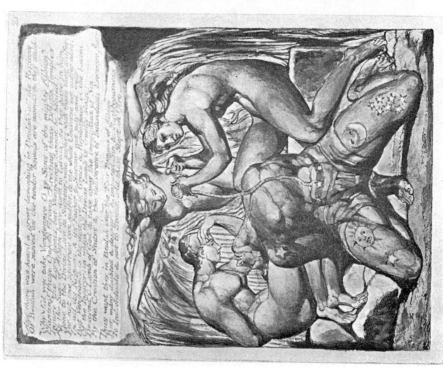

LVIII A　Blake, *Jerusalem*

And One spoed forth from the Divine Family & said

I feel my Spectre rising upon me! Albion, arouze thyself!
Why cast thou thunder with frozen Spectrous wrath against us?
The Spectre is in Giant Man; insane, and most deform'd
Thou wilt certainly provoke my Spectre against thine in fury!
He has a Sepulcher hewn out at a Rock ready for thee:
And a Death of Eight thousand years forg'd by thyself, upon
The point of his Spear! if thou persistest to forbid with Laws
Our Emanations; and to attack our secret supreme delights

So Los spoke: But when he saw blue death in Albions feet,
Again he joind the Divine Body following merciful;
While Albion fled more indignant; revengeful covering

LIX Blake, *Jerusalem*

LX   Blake, *Jerusalem*

All Human Forms identified even Tree Metal Earth & Stone. all
Human Forms identified. living going forth & returning wearied
Into the Planetary lives of Years Months Days & Hours, reposing
And then Awaking into his Bosom in the Life of Immortality.
And I heard the Name of their Emanations they are named Jerusalem

The End of The Song
of Jerusalem

LXI   Blake, *Jerusalem*

LXII B Blake, *Jerusalem*

LXII A Blake, *Jerusalem*

LXIII   Blake, *Night-Thoughts*

LXIV   Blake, *Night-Thoughts*

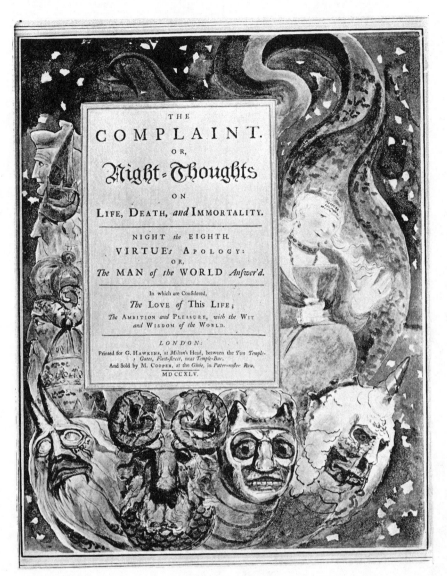

THE
COMPLAINT.
OR,
Night-Thoughts
ON
LIFE, DEATH, and IMMORTALITY.

NIGHT the EIGHTH.
VIRTUE's APOLOGY:
OR,
The MAN of the WORLD Answer'd.

In which are Considered,
The LOVE of This LIFE;
The AMBITION and PLEASURE, with the WIT
and WISDOM of the WORLD.

LONDON:
Printed for G. HAWKINS, at Milton's Head, between the Two Temple-
Gates, Fleet-street, near Temple-Bar.
And Sold by M. COOPER, at the Globe, in Pater-noster Row,
MDCCXLV.

LXV Blake, *Night-Thoughts*

LXVI b   Blake, *Night-Thoughts*

LXVI a   Blake, *Night-Thoughts*

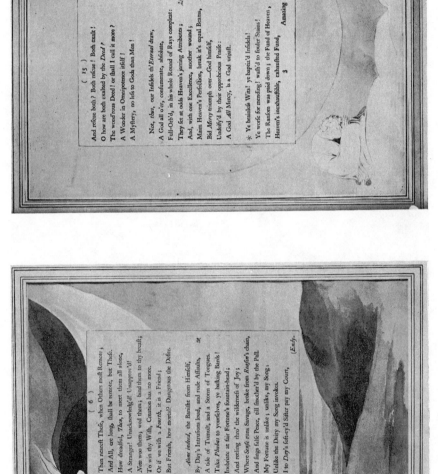

LXVII A   Blake, *Night-Thoughts*

LXVII B   Blake, *Night-Thoughts*

LXVIII Blake, *L'Allegro*

LXIX Blake, *Comus*

LXX   Blake, *Inferno*

LXXI Blake, *Paradise Lost*

LXXII Blake, *Paradise Lost*

LXXIII   Blake, "Elohim Creating Adam"

LXXIV Blake, *Job*

The Fire of God is fallen from Heaven

And the Lord said unto Satan Behold All that he hath is in thy Power

3

Thy Sons & thy Daughters were eating & drinking Wine in their
eldest Brothers house &: behold there came a great wind from the Wilderness
& smote upon the four faces of the house & it fell upon the young Men & they are Dead

W Blake invent & sculp

London, Published as the Act directs March 8. 1825 by W Blake N 3 Fountain Court Strand

Proof

LXXV   Blake, *Job*

LXXVI   Blake, *Job*

Then a Spirit paſed before my face
the hair of my flesh stood up

LXXVII Blake, *Job*

II

My bones are pierced in me in the night season & my sinews take no rest

My skin is black upon me & my bones are burned with heat

The triumphing of the wicked is short, the joy of the hypocrite is but for a moment

Satan himself is transformed into an Angel of Light & his Ministers into Ministers of Righteousness

With Dreams upon my bed thou scarest me & affrightest me with Visions

Why do you persecute me as God & are not satisfied with my flesh. Oh that my words were printed in a Book that they were graven with an iron pen & lead in the rock for ever For I know that my Redeemer liveth & that he shall stand in the latter days upon the Earth & after my skin destroy thou This body yet in my flesh shall I see God whom I shall see for Myself and mine eyes shall behold & not Another tho consumed be my wrought Image

Who opposeth & exalteth himself above all that is called God or is Worshipped

W Blake invent & sculp

London Published as the Act directs March 8 1825 by Will Blake N Fountain Court Strand

LXXVIII   Blake, *Job*

LXXIX Blake, *Job*

Great & Marvellous are thy Works Lord God Almighty

Just & True are thy Ways O thou King of Saints

So the Lord blessed the latter end of Job
more than the beginning

After this Job lived
an hundred & forty years
& saw his Sons & his
Sons Sons

In burnt Offerings for Sin

thou hast had no Pleasure

even four Generations
So Job died
being old
& full of days

W Blake inv & sculp

London Published as the Act directs March 8: 1825 by William Blake Fountain Court Strand

LXXX Blake, *Job*

Index